PRAISE FOR *WHY WAIT?*

"*Why Wait?* Is a timely, thought provoking page-turner that should be considered a desk reference for caregivers and those who would be caregivers of all ages. Thank you, Carolyn Brent!"
—Rawle Andrews, Jr., Esq., Regional Vice President, AARP

"Carolyn Brent's book is a personal, compelling account of not only her own story but also the stories of other family caregivers faced with difficult sibling issues. It is thorough, accurate, and highly credible. Brent has taken her own painful experience, summarized what might have been done differently as a lesson for others, and put it all together with compassion and understanding. Her straightforward advice can serve as an excellent help to anyone in the situation of working with siblings on parent care. She teaches us all through her own, well written story. I highly recommend it!"
—Carolyn L. Rosenblatt, R.N., attorney, author of *The Boomer's Guide to Aging Parents*

"As a pastor, former pastor to pastors, and a counselor, I endorse Carolyn Brent's book as an excellent resource. Also I recommend it for inclusion in all church libraries, in the homes of people who are caregivers for loved ones, and in the offices of pastors and others who work with people who care for aging parents and others. This book will change the lives of family caregivers and it will provide essential information for those who make the lives of loved ones as comfortable as possible. Carolyn shares her soul, her heart, and herself with the world in a way that will bring about crucial, positive change in the lives of those who take care of family and friends."
—Rev. Dr. Mary Newbern-Williams, Pastor, Cote Brilliante Presbyterian Church (St. Louis, Missouri)

"It takes real courage to reveal your darkest hour and your deepest vulnerability to benefit others. Carolyn Brent is truly inspirational. Her book offers us the universal wisdom of her life lessons. *Why Wait?* has set a new, elevated standard for turning adversity in life to love and redemption."

—Mikol Davis, Ph.D., geriatric psychologist, CEO of AgingParents.com

"As a pastor, physician, veteran, and one who was also a caregiver and suffered loss, I know Carolyn Brent has stripped the cover off of one of life's most painful processes. *Why Wait?* challenges us to take an honest look at our deepest fears and rejoice in our hope of true reconciliation."

—Charles Woodridge, M.D.

"Carolyn Brent has so eloquently created a life changing gift for our society with her groundbreaking book, *Why Wait?* Until now, we have had to walk through the challenging maze of caring for our aging parents alone and now, with Carolyn's dynamic insight and invaluable support, we can prepare mentally, emotionally, and strategically to make these years the absolute best they can be. I highly recommend this book."

—Allison Maslan, President, Allison Maslan International, author of *Blast Off!*

"In *Why Wait?* Carolyn Brent boldly addresses all the topics nobody wants to talk about, but absolutely must. This book is a goldmine of information not only for Baby Boomers facing the challenges of caring for their own parents, but also for children of us Baby Boomers as we begin to replace our parents as the older generation."

—Lynn Serafinn, marketer, coach, author of *The Garden of the Soul* and *The 7 Graces of Marketing*

Why Wait?

*The Baby Boomers' Guide to Preparing
Emotionally, Financially and Legally
for a Parent's Death*

CAROLYN A. BRENT, M.B.A.

Grandpa's Dream LLC
San Ramon, California

ISBN-10 0615475019

ISBN-13 9780615475011

Website: www.CaregiverStory.com

Email: Carolyn@CaregiverStory.com

1. Aging Parents 2. Family Relationships 3. Self-help 4. Home Care 5. Alzheimer's Disease 6. Financial Planning 7. Legal Planning 8. Death and Dying

Cover Design: Renee Duran
Interior Design: Shaila Abdullah
Editor: Stephanie Gunning
Photography of the white American pelican: © Ron Boily
Photography of the Sonoma Beach State Park: © Grant Kinney

DEDICATION

To my dad, Pastor William L. Brent, Th.D.
I thank God to have been blessed with him, as the
most wonderful parent I could have ever hoped for.

CONTENTS

PREFACE

MY DAD AND I WERE VERY CLOSE. AS A SINGLE parent, he raised me from the age of twelve to nineteen, the age at which I left home. That year I moved from Denver to Los Angeles to explore what the world had to offer me. Dad remarried and we remained close. Over the years, I'd look forward to his visits to Los Angeles to celebrate his birthday with me each March. We would catch up and talk about a wide range of subjects during these visits. Since Dad was a church pastor, among other things he used our special time together to share the word of God with me.

As long as I live, I'll never forget one of his birthday visits. I decided to take Dad to Redondo Beach on a Wednesday afternoon. Hardly any people were around, and the day was beautiful. The ocean was misty and the Moon had risen and was hanging above us in the sky. Dad and I walked along the beach for a while until we found a comfortable spot to sit in the sand. Then, as we sat gazing at the water and listening to the calls of the seagulls and pelicans that were gracefully flying by us, he began to talk to me about God's love for humanity.

Pointing to one pelican slowly soaring high in the sky silhouetted against the Moon, Dad said, "Carolyn, do you see that pelican? Imagine if that beautiful bird had only one responsibility in life. What if it had to fly to the Moon and drop off a single grain of sand that it was carrying in its pouch, and then it had to repeat this task until all of the sand was removed from the face of the Earth?" Looking directly at me, he asked, "How long do you think it would take?"

"It would take forever," I answered.

"The love of God and my love for you are eternal," he said. "Even after I've gone to Glory, for as long as it would take a pelican to remove the sand from the Earth a grain at a time, that's how long my love will be with you."

That was the first time I can recall Dad speaking with me about the prospect of his death. Of course, I didn't really want to discuss it and, in fact, I think I changed the subject. Being in my twenties, death seemed far off. On some level, I felt that Dad would live forever and nothing bad could ever happen to him. But I also made a vow to God on that day that I'd always be there to take care of Dad if he needed me. He was my best friend, my hero, and my adviser, and I hoped and prayed he'd be with me forever. Later on, I did my best to honor this promise.

The good times I had with my dad continued for the next thirty-three years, and there were many opportunities for us to discuss his end-of-life wishes. We did the best we could to prepare. But when I became his caregiver, I discovered that knowing someone's wishes is not enough. Even doing paperwork is not always enough to protect an elderly parent and a family caregiver, particularly if other family members disagree with the arrangements that have been made. Even if you try to do the right things and do your best to prepare for every possible scenario that might arise, the chronic illness of a parent and the costs associated with it are challenging to manage.

INTRODUCTION
Talk Early, Talk Often

WHEN PARENTS ARE RAISING CHILDREN, THEY often speak with them about the great things they can accomplish in life, and help them to develop plans to achieve their dreams. Parents and children plan ahead and make decisions about graduation, where to go to college, career paths, weddings, births, family vacations, and retirement. Probably you can remember having those kinds of planning discussions with your parents. But think about the last time a discussion of end-of-life issues and death came up at your family dinner table as a future plan. Did it ever?

If you've never spoken with your parents about death and dying, you are not alone. Even when people do talk about such things, often the right documents aren't put in place to ensure people's desires are carried through. Nearly 55 percent of the American population has neither a living trust nor a will in place explaining how they'd prefer their medical, financial, and legal affairs be managed at the end of their lives. They haven't made choices about what happens if they're sick or dying, like who should pay their bills and oversee their medical treatment; they also haven't given their chosen advocates the legal authority to make decisions on their behalf.

Obviously there are big issues of denial going on in our society. Although no plans are set in place for death, death is guaranteed. Sooner or later our aging parents will die—and so will we.

Why Family Conversations Are Crucial

According to *Senior Journal,* there are over 79 million Baby Boomers in the United States. Baby Boomers are people born between 1946 and 1964. The parents of Boomers in their late forties have reached their sixties and seventies. Boomers in their sixties have parents already in their eighties and nineties. The point is, if you're a Boomer, then preparing emotionally, financially, and legally for your aging parent's end-of-life needs and death is increasingly relevant. The need for planning has become even more imperative than it was in decades past because our aging population is living longer, but not necessarily healthier; meaning, we are confronting a different set of medical concerns and choices than our forbears did.

For the elderly, now is the time for conversations about end-of-life issues to take place with their children, not later. And if your parents don't bring the subject up, as a concerned child you should. I call these conversations "crucial" because the outcome matters. I like the definition of a crucial conversation in the book *Crucial Conversations* by Kerry Patterson, Joseph Grenny, Ron McMillan, and Al Switzler (McGraw-Hill, 2002). These co-authors say a crucial conversation is one in which opinions may vary, stakes are high, and emotions run strong. Tough issues are being addressed and the results have a huge impact on your quality of life. If crucial conversations are done effectively, they transform lives and can help a family to bond.

Why wait to begin talking? Why wait until there is a crisis? It is much better to hold these crucial conversations early when your parents are still healthy and can articulate their wishes, needs, and concerns. When a family has a plan, it is much easier to work together as a team.

My Caregiver Story

I became an accidental expert on end-of-life plans and caregiving due to circumstances. For years, I tried unsuccessfully to talk with my siblings about the medical and financial needs of our aging father, then in his seventies, who was suffering from dementia and a variety of other health problems. I felt I should initiate the conversation because of my close relationship with Dad. Growing up, I lived with him, though not all of my siblings did. My family is quite large. My twin sister and I were fourth-born among eight siblings, seven from the same mother. When I was twelve years old, my parents divorced. I followed my father to his new home and lived with him until I graduated from high school. My twin sister was raised by my mother, along with our three elder brothers and one younger sister then alive. When I was nineteen and had already left home, our father remarried and my youngest sibling was born.

There were many reasons why I decided to live with my father when I was a teen. I truly believe he saved my life by helping me escape a dysfunctional household headed by my mom, in which it was hard for me to thrive. I was fortunate in doing so, as he became my greatest ally, my dearest friend, and my spiritual role model. My siblings did not have the same experience with my dad as I did, which meant that, unfortunately, the turbulent history of our family would prove to be an immense obstacle to communication when it mattered most.

As an adult, before Dad got sick, my brothers and sisters and I were adults living separate lives in different parts of the country; in contact, and yet not particularly intimate. In 1998, our widowed father was living alone in Colorado when I discovered that he was not eating properly and seemed confused. Upon examination by a doctor, he was diagnosed as being in the early stages of dementia. After flying back and forth to Colorado on a regular basis for a couple of years in order to help him manage his affairs, he agreed to move into my home in California, where I could care for him more attentively and contribute to his well-being on a daily basis.

I felt it was important to share the details of our father's medical condition with my siblings, so I put together a complete binder containing several years of medical and financial records that would make it possible for us to mutually track our father's history. I sent each of my brothers and sisters a copy of this five-inch binder by Federal Express for their review. However, after they got copies of the binder, all of them asked me just to handle it, saying they did not want to get involved. As the only sibling among us who had no children, I guess they must have assumed I had extra time and the resources necessary to care for Dad. True, I did have some resources. I was doing well in my career and prospering financially. I owned a nice house with enough space for him to live with me. Whatever their reasons, my siblings flat-out refused to have the crucial conversations with me, each other, and our father that adult children really need to have regarding an aging and ailing parent's health and affairs. They were simply too busy with their own lives, and so we put off talking. In our family, this led to an extremely bad outcome.

My dad was a decorated veteran who earned a purple heart in Korea. As a veteran, he was entitled to receive disability benefits from the federal government. Once his medical needs increased beyond the scope of my ability to care for him physically, I placed him in a private care facility. There his monthly expenses continued to increase as his medical needs increased. Only through a combination of social security benefits, Veterans Administration (VA) benefits, and paying cash out of my pocket, did we manage to pay for his care.

Conflicts arose between me and my siblings when it reached the point where they thought our father was dying. Then, all of a sudden it seemed to me, they wanted to be involved. They took me to court. For me, this was the beginning of a nightmarish chain of events. My twin sister was able to get a restraining order against me, forbidding me from visiting Dad without supervision. She got a judge to agree to this by making allegations in court—false allegations—that Dad was dying because of how I cared for him when he lived in my household, and because my other siblings got on board with her.

The basis of her claim was that at one point Dad took a fall while out jogging. Though his condition was deteriorating at the time, he could still function well enough back then to lead a fairly active life. However, this fall later on led him to develop hydrocephalus, a condition commonly known as "water on the brain," which played a role in the dementia he was experiencing. My sister used that fact as part of her evidence against me.

After being dragged through courts in several jurisdictions, including a probate court, our father was ultimately placed on welfare to cover his medical expenses. My dad did not die. He's alive and residing in a care facility. My siblings are in charge of his affairs. Since then, I've watched from afar as Dad's condition has worsened. I am angry and sad, and concerned, because it is the quality of the end of his life that is at stake—and because it really did not have to be this way. Given the option, I would gladly have continued being his primary caregiver. I miss him.

Having a crucial conversation or series of conversations as a family might have spared my siblings and I from discord. Instead of fighting, we could have created an opportunity for healing and resolving our relationships, and developed a strategy together where we pooled our resources to plan for, and manage, the challenges of our aging father's illness. As sad as chronic and progressive illness is to face when a parent is undergoing them, through active discussions greater clarity and mutual decision-making about finances and medical care can occur.

When a parent—or anyone, for that matter—reaches the end of life, there needs to be a way provided for that person to die with dignity and in relative peace. For children, this can be a difficult transition during which confusion and strife are not optimal.

Through struggling with the legal, medical, financial, and familial issues that come up when adult children handle such matters poorly (whether due to denial or to strife), I discovered there were no books on what needs to be covered and planned for, written from the perspective of siblings. Siblings have special needs at such times and, ideally, can be of great comfort to one another. I found no books that discussed the ideal scenario of sibling conversations versus the worst-case scenario of no conversations, as well as cases when sibling rivalry and resentment are allowed to interfere with planning and care. My siblings and I are living proof that this can go very, very wrong, leading to no one's benefit: neither the children's, nor the parent's.

The more research I did, the more committed I became to spreading the important message that planning is critical, and families must begin talking to one another as early as possible. For the past few years I've traveled across the country giving lectures at churches and to members of organizations with an interest in these issues, and I've spoken with numerous family caregivers. I set up CaregiverStory.com to disseminate resources to help family caregivers. I've gone on radio and television. I've worked to pass new laws in Congress. Now I've written *Why Wait?*

What This Book Covers

My goal in this book is to offer you insight as to why it is crucial for adult children to have conversations with their aging parents while the parents are still relatively healthy. These crucial conversations should cover the issue of what to do if a parent becomes disabled or ill and requires caregiving, and how to manage the parent's estate when they die. Perhaps the greatest need I intend to address in this book is the need for appropriate documentation. A parent needs to put in place an advance medical directive and a living trust, establish a will, and appoint an executor for his or her estate. In this book, I'll explain what is expressed by those documents and why they are necessary. I'll also expose the pitfalls of not preparing this type of documentation.

Grown siblings also need to have conversations with one another about caregiving for an aging parent. Obviously age alone is not the reason children would need to step in and begin to manage a parent's life. A healthy elderly person does not require a caregiver. However, the need for family caregiving typically increases as the parent ages, and in responding to that need siblings should ideally work together. In this book, I'll cover issues that children who are their parents' family caregivers often face, like dividing the workload, sibling rivalry, and handling disagreements. Sometimes siblings refuse to participate in caregiving or cannot be counted upon for support because of a problem in their own lives, such as addiction or disease.

If your aging parent selected you as his or her primary caregiver, you may find yourself in the position of needing to protect your parent—and yourself—from abusive, avaricious, or deceitful siblings. There are steps you can take to help your parent prevent his or her health and finances from being negatively impacted by the behavior of unscrupulous or misguided family members.

Too often, families postpone having crucial conversations about the "what ifs" of illness, old age, and death, and planning a course of action that covers the possibilities, until they're faced with a sudden acute need. Life can be clipping along at its usual pace, and then, out of the blue, an emergency call comes in. A senior parent has been rushed to the emergency room for a life-saving operation, or has fallen and broken a hip, or there's been a diagnosis of Alzheimer's disease. Now the children have to respond. But what should be done? Where are the financial records? Who has access to the bank accounts? What is the right medical treatment? Where is the parent going to live after this? How much support is needed and who is available to offer it? In an emergency, all of this confusion can be going on at the same time family members are feeling flooded by emotions like fear, sadness, and even anger because their lives are being disrupted.

One of the greatest tragedies can be when a family is not prepared and its members disagree about who should be in control of money, medicine, and care. Especially when relationships in a family are already rocky, an emergency could just be the beginning of a series of conflicts that arise over the steps that should be taken in the care of senior parents. Hurt feelings and fighting can be avoided if siblings and parents hold in-depth family conferences well before an emergency.

Even when siblings are not at odds, caregiving usually comes to rest on the shoulders of one person more than any other. Being a primary caregiver adds stress to your life. In this book, I'll cover what you can do to take good care of yourself if you are playing this important role.

Due to the pain of my experiences as a family caregiver at odds with her siblings, I am a strong believer that children and parents must talk early and often about issues related to aging and dying. It is best if everyone within the circle of an immediate family clearly understands each other's wishes and plans, even if some are not going to play an active role in caregiving. These conversations are essential for family members to become good partners for each other and strong advocates for each others' wishes when the end of life is approaching.

Baby Boomers really need to set their own affairs in order, as much as help their elderly parents handle theirs, particularly if parents are in some manner dependent upon the children. Just as young parents make decisions to protect their minor children, adult children should make provisions to protect their elderly parents in case something happens and the children are no longer around. Odds are that the older person will die first; but sometimes the younger one does. We Baby Boomers are not tender spring chickens. We're more like tough, old birds ourselves.

Once the necessary legal documents have been put in place, you and your siblings can get on with the important work of caregiving and, ultimately, saying goodbye to your parent. Preparation gives you room to grieve and a chance to come together for mutual solace and the celebration of your parent's life. Though the crucial conversations may feel uncomfortable, when your parent's death is near you'll be glad you had them, did the paperwork, and hopefully found a way to resolve past upsets, as this will free your energy for the beautiful emotional aspects of the experience, like giving and receiving love. In the end, love is the true essence and gift of a family united by a common purpose.

1

WHEN YOUR PARENT CAN NO LONGER LIVE ALONE

MY FATHER LIVED WITH HIS SECOND WIFE UNTIL she passed away in 1998. Before his retirement, he ran a ministry in the small, rural town of Lamar, Colorado, which is located 200 miles east of Denver and has a population of 8,000 people. The church ended when he stopped working. After his wife's death, he lived a quiet life and fell out of touch with the people in his community. We were in frequent contact, but I didn't know anything was wrong until one day when he called me very upset.

"Carolyn," he requested, "can you come help me?" Someone had run into the back of Dad's car, wrecking it, and he didn't know what to do. He needed to buy a new car and couldn't handle the insurance paperwork on his own. Though he wasn't physically injured, he was emotionally frazzled and overwhelmed. I flew out and took charge.

A few months later, I got another similar call from Dad. He'd accidentally left a hose on and water had flooded his basement.

He needed assistance in coping with the steps of making a homeowner's insurance claim. Again, I did the paperwork for him.

Before Dad moved to California to live with me, I traveled the country regularly for my job as a clinical education manager in the pharmaceutical industry. This allowed me frequent opportunities to visit him at his home in Colorado. When I discovered on these visits that he was losing weight, seemed depressed, and clearly was not his usual self, I knew it was time for me to become more involved. I suggested he come live with me. He didn't agree immediately.

The period in which I was taking care of my father from a distance was tough on me. I didn't realize it, but my role in my father's life was being transformed. Because Dad was losing weight, I brought him to see a doctor. The moment when the doctor praised me, saying, "It's so good you're his caregiver," was the moment I became conscious that *I was a caregiver.*

After a couple of years of flying back and forth to Colorado frequently, in 2000 Dad finally agreed to move into my home. I got a call from him when I was literally on my way to Florida for a national meeting of my company's sales managers. I phoned my boss and told her I would be late because I had to pick Dad up, and then diverted myself to Colorado. Dad had a tiny suitcase packed. He was ready to go as soon as I arrived. We flew together to California, where I got him settled in my home, and then I hopped on another flight to Florida.

A few weeks later, I flew back to Colorado once again, removed Dad's furniture and cleaned the house with the help of one of my brothers, went to see a realtor, and put Dad's house on the market. It sold six months later. Dad's transition to living in my home was complete.

The First Decision: Selection of a Primary Caregiver

The typical profile of a family caregiver in our society, after a spouse, is a grown daughter in her midlife who views caregiving as her social role. But family caregivers may be people of any age and gender. Grown sons often fall into this role if they are the sibling in their family living closest to the parent. And, of course, only children have no siblings with whom to share the responsibility. For different reasons, caregivers are the children who answer the call.

Being a primary caregiver is a huge responsibility. Law-Glossary.com defines a caregiver as the "person who is primarily responsible for looking after someone's health, safety and comfort." When speaking about aging adults, a primary caregiver steps in only when someone cannot *fully* care for himself or herself. A primary caregiver may be a selected family member, a medical professional in a care facility, or a trained professional living outside the home. In this book, we're focusing only on the grown children who assume this role on behalf of their parents.

For a period of time, caregiving can be offered to a parent from a distance while the parent remains in place in his or her own home. After a while, the parent's needs may increase to the point where living independently is problematic. Perhaps falls are periodically taking place or meals are being missed. Then other options will need to be considered and action taken.

When is the right time to make the decision to move an elderly parent into the home of a family member or an assisted-living environment? When the parent is no longer able to care for him or herself and live independently. Gauging whether or not the move into your home is appropriate depends on the level of care the parent needs, and what you are capable of handling. When it is evident that an elderly parent is at risk of harm unless they have twenty-four-hour help in meeting their everyday needs, then home care may be the right choice.

In my own situation, for instance, it was easier on me to have my elderly father living in my home than continuously having to travel to another state to care for him, as this caused less disruption to my life and livelihood. When an elderly parent lives with an offspring it can give the whole family peace of mind knowing that the parent is in a safe place with a loved one.

When you choose to provide care for an elderly parent in your own home, it is an act of unconditional love and loyalty that money cannot buy. No amount could compensate for the hard work involved in undertaking this responsibility when the care you give a parent is based upon the right motivations. No hired caregiver, no matter how well trained, could ever love your parent as much as you do. Your family truly needs to understand the significance of selecting the right caregiver, and the level of dedication that family caregiving demands.

Family discussions about future options for a parent's care should cover the important topic of selecting the *right* caregiver and putting the legal paperwork in place that solidifies the choice, as well as conversations on how to support the person taking on the responsibility. The selection should be based on qualifications and temperament, rather than on emotion. A child probably should not be selected when the individual does not have a peaceful relationship with the parent, is struggling financially, or behaves irresponsibly. Not if there is another option available.

Documenting the choice of a caregiver is essential, for reasons we'll explore in a later chapter. The courts are bulging with family disputes about parental care and the distribution of parental assets after death, when nothing has been established officially in writing. This is when the chances are greater for fights among siblings to erupt over the care of a parent. In the case of my family, I was appointed primary caregiver by my dad in his healthier years, and my siblings accepted this fact. However, we had put nothing about our arrangement in writing. If the decision is not put in writing, it does not exist in a court of law.

Fights do not necessarily mean siblings genuinely care about their parents' needs and wishes. In many cases, such legal battles are about financial gain. Sometimes they erupt over what siblings think they're entitled to, and how they want to "get onboard the gravy train" when they think a parent is dying.

If this sounds harsh, remember that my goal is to educate you on how to protect aging parents and their primary family caregivers. My focus is on how to make the end of your parent's life as peaceful as possible for everyone involved. My strong desire is that you and your siblings will pull together as a team when the time comes to care for a parent who requires assistance.

Making Caregiving a Family Affair

It is in the best interest of siblings to pull together as a team when there's a need to care for a chronically ill or dying parent. How different family members step in at such a time to offer assistance to the parent depends on the relationship dynamics of the family. Ultimately your role in your parent's care depends on many factors, not the least of which is your willingness to be involved, and whether or not your parent is competent to make decisions and desires your participation.

Here are some other considerations:

- Is the parent married or single?
- Is the parent's spouse capable of handling the needs of the situation?
- Are you an only child or do you have siblings?
- Are you and/or your siblings capable of handling the needs of the situation? Do you live close by? Do you have the knowledge or training required? Do you have the physical and emotional stamina required? Do you have the temperament and inclination to play this role? Do you have the financial resources required? Do you have the availability required?
- Do you get along with your parent?
- Do you get along with your parent's spouse?
- Do you and your siblings get along?

Families come in all shapes and sizes. Every family has its own relationship dynamics; its own values to confer; its own capabilities to rely upon; and its own medical, financial, and legal circumstances to contend with. For the purpose of this discussion of team-building, I'm making two fundamental assumptions: first, you've chosen to be involved in your parent's end-of-life planning and care, if that is needed and appropriate; second, you have your parent's best interests at heart.

To be clear, throughout this book I am particularly addressing the concerns of adult children, rather than the concerns of caregiver spouses, although the two areas of focus often overlap in the real world. Here, I am specifically covering the topic of sibling relationships, because only children will experience neither the potential benefits of sibling partnerships, nor the potential obstacles that are the outcome of sibling disagreements. If you are an only child and a caregiver, please be aware that you and your parent also need to prepare and that you will need support.

The end of life can be a challenging time. Typically, as people age, they need more assistance as their physical and cognitive abilities progressively diminish. But when an aging parent is in good health, there is no reason to aim to take over the management of his or her life. The decision of when it's appropriate for you to pitch in and help your healthy aging parent is really your parent's call to make. While you can offer support to a generally healthy parent, and it is, of course, kind and considerate to offer, you and your parent would both be better served to use the period of their good health to set a plan in place for the time it is needed, to enjoy each other's company, and, if there are unresolved issues or resentments in your relationship, to do your best to resolve them.

Should your parent's physical or mental health begin to decline precipitously, certain assessments need to be made. These pertain to the status of your parent's health, financial resources, and estate, and who in your family is best equipped to offer assistance. This is the time when your intervention in your parent's life may become necessary. If your family has already put a plan in place for how to handle your parent's affairs, you can simply set your plan into motion. If you haven't yet put a plan in place and an emergency arises, you'll need to look at these issues immediately. Having the proper paperwork in place can spare your family from facing all kinds of problems down the line. Furthermore, in the midst of a crisis is a lousy time to be distracted by the need to learn what to do.

Emotions often run high when a parent is seriously injured, chronically ill, or dying. If you are caught by surprise, this can be a frightening time. You may feel shock, and also grief, among other things. Siblings who come together in mutual support at times of acute need can be wonderful sources of solace for one another. You and your siblings share a history that bypasses the need for explanation. You can take turns lifting each other's spirits; taking care of different tasks related to the supervision of your parent's medical, legal, and financial affairs—as the case may be—as well as being present and available to your ailing parent and their spouse, who may or may not be your biological parent.

Even if one sibling is the parent's primary caregiver, caregiving is accomplished more effectively when it is a team effort. Taking on the responsibility of bringing a parent into your home is a great act of love. Caregiving consumes time, energy, and financial resources. Siblings of a primary caregiver can make the caregiver's life easier by providing emotional support, financial support, and the support of being present so the caregiver can take some time off. A caregiver would benefit from an occasional outing, a day at a spa, or just hearing a simple "thank you." It is very important to remind caregivers of how much they are appreciated.

In an effort to spread the care of a parent among siblings:

Divide up the tasks. If everyone takes on different responsibilities, the workload is lightened. For example, one child could handle medical aspects of care. Another child could handle financial aspects of care. Another could handle grocery shopping and/or meal preparation. Be sure to keep one another informed about the ongoing status in your own areas of responsibility, and mention changes you see in your parent to each other.

Settle on the primary caregiver. One sibling needs to hold the legal decision-making authority for the parent, and this role must ideally be established with documentation. It doesn't mean other siblings cannot contribute opinions, it only means that at the end of the day there is no confusion when your family is interacting with doctors.

Express your fears and concerns. Siblings can be a source of emotional comfort to one another. But you have to open up and share your thoughts and feelings for this to happen. You can't expect your siblings to guess what's going on with your parent, or how you're being impacted by your role as a caregiver unless you let them into your life.

Give up trying to be in control of everything. Regrettably, you won't get much sympathy for your stress about caretaking from your siblings if you are in the habit of doing everything for your parent yourself, and you won't let them help you although they've offered. Be willing to share the caregiver's role and understand that each of your siblings has a personal relationship with the parent that is uniquely theirs.

Have regular check-ins or conferences. Touch base with one another by phone on a regular basis. You can use a free computer-based phone system like Skype for a conference call, or get together in person if you live close enough. Or just hop on a phone bridge line like FreeConferenceCall.com. Staying in touch even if nothing urgent is going on strengthens the sibling bond. Use this as a time to laugh and share news about your lives, as well as information about your parent's condition. Being in touch on a weekly or monthly basis is one of the ways to help lighten each other's emotional load. People who feel isolated are more prone to depression and overwhelm. Just being heard and having a chance to self-express is like a safety relief valve on a pressure boiler: It lets you blow off steam.

Make specific, clear requests. In order to move into action you need to know who will do what, and by when, and how that action will be followed up. If you take time to assess your underlying needs and what you really want to happen, before asking for your siblings to take action, you will be able to articulate your request in a clear, specific way they can respond to. Become aware of the difference between a request and a *demand*. With a request, the response may either be a yes or a no, and that's acceptable. With a demand, a no answer is usually followed by a guilt-trip or rage. If you make a demand, a no is rebellion and a yes is submission. With a respectful request made of an equal, there are usually more possibilities available than a simple yes or no.

In general, family caregivers are not paid to do the work. However, they often change their work schedules or even quit their jobs so they can be present for a parent, and this can put a strain on their finances. In my own case, a few years later I would eventually change jobs, taking a sizable cut in my salary, so I could continue working, but as a sales rep in the local area around my home.

Keep in mind that the person most prone to burnout in a caregiving arrangement is the primary caregiver, which is why a caregiver deserves to be rewarded with your support in any form you can give it, including financially. You have the power to turn caregiving into a family affair by regularly making visits, calling, assisting with household tasks such as preparing meals, running errands, buying groceries, doing laundry, administering medications, and taking the aging parent to doctor's appointments or church. Teenage offspring can also be included in helping care for an elderly grandparent. The demands of care can be overwhelming if the primary caregiver doesn't have enough family or social support available.

In a family where one sibling is the primary caregiver, I recommend that everyone else volunteers at an assisted-living facility or nursing home for a day or a week, in order to experience the daily activities related to caregiving, and gain a clearer perspective of what is actually involved. The everyday care of your parent should not be left entirely to the primary caregiver simply because this child lives closest or has volunteered. In some cases, siblings may live in another state or country, at a distance that makes it difficult for them to contribute care to the parent. If you're far away, you might make a point of visiting for a week every year so the primary caregiver can take a vacation from the duties of caregiving.

When children are not involved in the routine care of a parent, they may not understand the changes the parent is undergoing. They may even be in denial that the parent actually has an illness, or is becoming less capable of managing his or her routine affairs. Often a decline in a parent's abilities is gradual. Sometimes it can be shocking when a non-participating child visits an elderly parent and discovers a big change has taken place. Especially after a major surgery or an illness, the change in a parent's mental condition and physical appearance can be downright shocking. This is the point when some primary caregivers find themselves in court being accused of elder abuse or neglect.

The need for you, your siblings, and your parent to plan for your parent's future needs is imperative. You should talk about medical plans, financial resources, naming a fiduciary, and setting up a living trust in order for your parent to receive the best possible care—in the form that is desired by the parent—and so that an agreed-upon plan of action will be followed by the family members who choose to be involved. You can even create a formal sibling contract that puts agreements in writing. We'll cover types of documents that need to be put in place in the chapter on legal issues (Chapter 6).

Chronic illnesses like Alzheimer's disease only worsen with the passage of time; they never improve. As the quality of your parent's health declines and the need for a variety of medical interventions increases, more care may ultimately be required than you are capable of providing for the parent in your own home. That's when the option of assisted living or a nursing home enters the picture.

You must carefully weigh the advantages and disadvantages of bringing a parent to live with you. As your parent's health worsens you could find yourself in over your head. Some elderly people are difficult to deal with. Especially when suffering from dementia, they can become irritable and overly demanding due to changes in their mental state. At night, their confusion may be more intense. They can even be delusional. This phenomenon is known as *sundowner's syndrome.* Symptoms can be dangerous both for the person with the illness and for anyone around them. When a parent reaches the point where they wander off and get lost, they are at risk of victimization from strangers. The elderly parent is now in a situation where he or she must be supervised twenty-four hours a day, seven days a week.

New choices must be made when you reach this point in caregiving. If you wish to keep the elderly parent at home, you can hire someone to help you manage your responsibilities. But you must make decisions based on what is best for everyone living in your household, taking into consideration both your parent's health and safety, and the well-being and safety of other family members, including yourself, the primary caregiver. Often, it is a sudden acute need or an emergency that disrupts your routine that serves as a signal about a new problem looming on the horizon.

2

MOVING YOUR PARENT INTO AN ASSISTED-LIVING FACILITY OR NURSING HOME

SEVERAL MONTHS INTO OUR NEW LIVING arrangement in California, Dad appeared to me to be okay for the most part. Sure he would sometimes forget whether or not he'd taken his different medications and where he placed his car keys, but I didn't look at his forgetfulness as a big deal. You wouldn't have known he had any problems if you interacted with him. Ever pragmatic, I thought, *I can be in charge of monitoring Dad's medication. I'll have an extra set of car keys made in case he loses his again. No problem.* Frankly, I was wrong about the scope of his needs.

One evening, as I arrived home and was parking my car in the driveway, I noticed Dad seated in the courtyard in his favorite chair outside the house. He had an unusual look on his face. His skin appeared to have darkened. His eyes were glazed like he was staring off into space. After I touched him and got his attention, I noticed a burning smell coming from inside the house. I ran inside and found a pot of pinto beans on fire in the kitchen. Thank God

I was able to put out the flames. Unfortunately, smoke had permeated the entire house by the time I got there! Until it faded many weeks later, we had to tolerate a horrible burnt aroma.

Yes, Dad was cooking. He'd been making one of his favorite foods on the stove and forgotten what he was doing. The oddest part was when he told me, "I don't know who was in your kitchen cooking." Since it was just the two of us living in my home, I thought he must be joking and let the matter drop for a while.

After several cooking incidents like this took place, I realized I needed help. No longer just my father's daughter, I was also his caregiver and recognized that it was a huge responsibility. First, I reached out to my siblings and asked them to help in any way they could by making regular visits, calling Dad on the telephone, cooking meals, taking Dad to the doctor, and so on. A few of them lived near enough that visiting would have been possible. Regrettably for Dad and myself, they made it clear to me that they were too busy with their own lives to pitch in.

Next, I contacted my church for support in managing our challenges. The senior pastor made some recommendations. Following his advice, I hired a man from the church to make meals for Dad during the week while I was at work, and also to transport him to and from a nearby senior center. The assistance I received from this man and the center was essential to the quality of our lives. It gave me the peace of mind to know Dad had others looking out for him besides me.

We lived together like this for approximately two years. I always remembered that my father had told me, "You are God's special child." More than once he had remarked, "I trust you with my life and I want you to take care of me if anything should happen."

I felt honored to help him. Though I was still unaware of the severity of the medical conditions he was developing, I also worried all of the time that if I wasn't around something bad would happen.

In December 2001, as I was boarding an airplane in Burbank to return to Northern California after an eight-hour business trip, I received a call from a hospital saying my father had taken a fall while jogging and had been injured. Boy, that seventy-five-minute flight seemed as if it was years long! I couldn't get to the hospital fast enough. Once the plane landed in Sacramento, I had an additional hour of driving to do to reach the emergency room. Every moment that passed seemed like an eternity. Once at the ER, I hugged all of the staff members and thanked them for caring for my father and watching over him until I could arrive. Because he had only a couple of stitches on his forehead and some abrasions on his face, they had not been obligated to keep him at the hospital. I remember pleading with the nurse I spoke with on the phone to keep my father with them and not release him until I got there, explaining to her that I feared he could hurt himself if he was traveling alone and still feeling shaky.

Fortunately, things were fine after that for a couple years more, as long as I kept a close eye on him. He went to the senior center where he played cards with his friends and occasionally gave talks on spiritual topics. He came to church with me on Sundays. He participated in life at home and in the company of my friends. We settled into a routine that felt manageable.

One spring day in 2002, in the late afternoon, my father stuck his head through the door of the home office where I was working. "Carolyn Ann," he asked, "would you like me to pick anything up for you while I'm at the store?" It was normal for him to drive himself a few blocks down the street to the grocery store to pur-chase sweets and other things he enjoyed eating—a non-event, so to speak.

My reply was, "No thank you, Dad. Get what you need and I'll see you soon. By the time you get back, dinner will be ready. I love you." A few minutes after he left, I started dinner. Twenty minutes passed. I felt myself growing concerned, but dismissed it. *Carolyn, quit being such a worrywart! Dad will be home in a few minutes.*

Then I remember how I started nervously pacing back and forth in the living room while looking out the large picture win-dow. I was waiting for Dad to turn the corner, drive down the street, and park his car in our driveway. By the time an hour had gone by I was genuinely worried. I hopped into my car and drove to the grocery store as quickly as I could. Once there, I slowly drove past every parked car in the parking lot, looking for his ve-hicle. There was no sign of him or his car anywhere. Thinking someone had possibly seen him, I parked my car. I went into the store and spoke with the employees. I described Dad and what he was wearing: a hat, a polo shirt, and navy blue slacks. Everyone told me the same thing, "Sorry, I haven't seen your father. But I wish you good luck in finding him."

After getting this disheartening news, I rushed back to my car and drove home to see if Dad had made it back while I was out. My chief anxiety was that he'd had an accident. I hoped we'd some-how passed by each other and that he was safe and sound, waiting for me. But this was not the case. When I arrived home, I still saw no parked car and no Dad.

Panic began to set in. *Where is my dad? This is not like him! He always goes to the grocery store without any trouble.* As the sun began to set, my heart pounded harder and faster. The thought of my father lost or hurt somewhere out in the darkness was terrifying.

When I couldn't wait any longer, I called the local police and the state highway patrol and asked for their assistance in finding Dad. After explaining what had happened earlier—that Dad had told me he'd be right back and hadn't returned, and I'd searched for him along his route—they took a description and said they'd keep an eye out for him. My mind flashed to the tragic missing-person TV shows I'd viewed, dramatizing situations I hoped I'd never experience.

Later that evening, I received a telephone call from a woman who worked at a car dealership in Sacramento. I remember how she asked me if I knew a Mr. Brent. She was concerned because it appeared as if he'd urinated in his pants. When he asked her for directions to his daughter's home, she'd requested my telephone number so she could speak with me. She told me that she'd given Dad written instructions and then he'd left the dealership and headed home. I told her, "Oh yes! That's my father. Thank you for calling. Oh thank you! Please keep him there."

"Oh no, he's not here anymore," she replied. "He left about five minutes ago."

"Please run out to see if you can catch him," I requested. The woman did, but it was too late. He was gone. Not knowing what else to do, I got into my car and drove the ninety miles to the car dealership in Sacramento. By the time I got there, it was closed for the evening. If Dad was really as disoriented as he sounded, I didn't believe he would have made it far. I wanted to be close by when he was located.

On the way to Sacramento I had phoned the highway patrol with my new information and Dad was placed on a statewide missing persons list. In Sacramento, I drove up and down the streets in the area around the car dealership looking for Dad. I stopped at 7-Eleven stores and gas stations where he might stop. No one had seen him.

Feeling my panic rising again, I placed a call to my best friend, Thell, in Los Angeles, asking her to say or do something to calm me down. Thell prayed with me and expressed her concern for my safety. Then she begged me to go home and wait. "Baby," she said, "you can drive back to Sacramento in the morning to look for your father, but please, Carolyn, go home now and wait." I took her advice and drove home hoping things would change for the better by the morning.

At two in the morning I received a telephone call from my dad. He was calling me from a payphone. He said, "Carolyn, I'm looking for your house. Can you give me some directions?"

I asked, "Dad, where are you?"

"I don't really know where I am," he replied.

"Do you see anyone or anything near you?" I asked, thinking I could figure out how to come and get him.

As Dad responded, "I think there is a store across the road," I started perspiring and my heart began racing. I was thinking, *Thank you, God, for finding my father,* when all of a sudden I heard a dial tone. I panicked as I heard the thump-thump of my heart pounding loudly in my chest. *Oh my god, he never told me where he was!*

I immediately called the highway patrol again and told them about my dad's call, and how we disconnected. The officer on duty told me he could trace the call and would find my dad for me—

not to worry. Within twenty minutes he called me back and told me my dad was doing fine. An officer had found Dad, and Dad had followed him back to the patrol station where he was now drinking hot coffee. I heard the officer tell Dad, "Your daughter is on her way to pick you up." They argued. Dad sounded resistant to this idea; apparently he only wanted the officer to give him directions to drive home. The police didn't think this was a good idea. It turned out that Dad was nearly 150 miles away in Yuba City, a small town I'd never heard of before.

After driving two-and-a-half hours, I entered the highway patrol station and ran over to hug Dad. He was not a happy camper. Clearly he was upset that he'd been made to wait in the station for me against his will. Dad didn't grasp that he was on the missing persons list or understand what I'd been going through emotionally back at home, or that I had been driving around for hours searching for him.

That night was the first time I was able to see for certain that Dad was in the early stages of dementia. His condition was more problematic than forgetting to turn off the stove or not being able to remember what medications he'd taken. I saw a person in front of me whom I did not recognize. Now I understood that I was dealing with a disease I needed to learn more about.

As Dad and I drove home in my car from Yuba City, I felt as if I was driving home with a stranger. Among other things, for the first time in my life I heard my dad curse, which shocked me. He had saliva foaming at the corners of his mouth and the shadows of a partial white beard on his chin and cheeks. I was dismayed at seeing my dad like this because he was always fastidious about his appearance and a well-dressed man.

When we got home, it was already past daybreak. I helped Dad get into bed and he began to curse at me again. I knew he truly needed help, and I knew I needed help, so I decided to call the local Veterans Administration Hospital. After sharing the story of the previous twenty-four-hour period with the advice nurse, she told me she would send a team from the VA to my home in order to evaluate my Dad, to see what kind of medical intervention would be necessary.

A few hours later, two men from the behavioral healthcare department came to our home. When they asked Dad a couple of questions, he became agitated. He cursed at the men and demanded they leave. I was stunned. Dad's condition was clearly worsening. I walked the VA staff members out to their car and asked them what they thought I should do. They told me Dad needed immediate medical attention and that he was at risk for wandering and getting lost again. "Next time you may not be as lucky in finding him."

I asked them what their recommendation was as the next step. They both said, "You must think of a way to bring him to the St. Joseph's Behavioral Health Center." One added, "Keep in mind that your dad needs to get his medication adjusted in order to keep him safe."

After bringing my dad to St. Joseph's Behavioral Health Center the next day, I was faced with the prospect of moving him into an assisted-living facility. This decision was extremely difficult for me, as it may be for you and your siblings. I felt guilty about making it. However, I also felt I had no choice if I wanted to ensure my dad's safety and based on his medical needs. Safety was my highest priority. At this point, because he was wandering and getting lost,

Dad required twenty-four-hour care, which was not possible for me to provide him on my own as a single working professional.

The Progression of Long-term Care

The progression of most elderly people through increasingly deeper levels of long-term care (LTC) is a gradual process. I liken this to the way an athlete comes to be recruited by the National Football League (NFL). Yes, the NFL. Although joining the NFL is an exciting path for an athlete and the path of LTC for a parent is obviously not, the steps are similar. Here's how:

In the game of football, there are different levels. Playing for an NFL team is what every young football player aspires to. To reach this level, kids start playing football in the streets with their friends. If they're lucky, they play Pop Warner football on the weekends. After that, they play high school football. Then, if they have enough talent, some get scholarships to play football in a college league. Some make the team as walk-on players. The dream is to be drafted into the NFL after graduation. When players show strong potential, but aren't ready to play in the ranks of NFL athletes, they're sent to play in the European league. When deemed ready, they come back to the U.S. and join the NFL. Of course, there are also athletes who never get there.

Before seniors reach the need for professional long-term care, they do whatever they can to remain independent. A home can be modified using principles of universal design to accommodate a reduction in physical ability. Avoiding trips and falls is an important factor in a senior remaining independent. With worsening eyesight, dim lighting can be dangerous and a loose rug can slide in a precarious way. Secure footing is an element of universal home design. So is having the ability to travel between different floors in a house. Some people install elevator seats to carry seniors up and down staircases. Putting handrails in the bathtub-shower area is useful. For a senior who uses a wheelchair or a scooter to get around, ramps become important features of the home. See the Recommended Resources section for more information on universal design.

When you see a parent having trouble meeting routine needs like doing laundry, making meals, and having frequent accidents, you know it's time to consider moving the parent into your own home where you can contribute care for them, or moving them into long-term care. As long as you are able to co-exist with your parent successfully, this option is appropriate. You can certainly add support to the in-home care you provide by hiring help or relying upon volunteers. But if your aging parent's condition has deteriorated seriously or an illness has advanced beyond a certain point, long-term care may be a better fit than home care.

Some elders in our society do not wish to "burden" their grown children by moving in with them. If a parent has the financial wherewithal to afford to live in an assisted-living community, he or she may choose to go directly there. Not everyone has the means to finance this choice. As you consider increasing levels of care, understanding how to pay for this service is critical. See the chapter entitled "Crucial Financial Conversations" (Chapter 5) for more details on various considerations.

Long-term care facilities have different levels, ranging from assisted-living centers, where each senior has a small apartment and receives meals in a common dining hall, and there is also a trained support staff regularly checking up on the residents; to around-the-clock nursing care facilities that resemble hospitals, and where constant medical care is provided.

A final option is one for the dying parent. Hospice care is something that can be given in a hospital, a home, or a private facility when the end of life is imminent. If your parent is terminally ill and wishes no further extreme medical interventions are taken on his or her behalf, hospice is often preferred because of the philosophy behind the treatment. Receiving food, water, and pain management continue in a hospice situation only for as long as they are requested. By contrast, doctors and hospitals often intervene to keep their patients alive right to the bitter end.

When you see your parent needing more assistance, you can:

1. Schedule a helper to come to the house to provide your parent in-home care.

2. Move your parent into an assisted-living residence that offers a relatively independent lifestyle, but trained personnel are on the premises. In the first level of assisted living residents are free to come and go as they please. In the second level of assisted living, such as would be needed by a patient in an advanced stage of dementia, for their own protection residents are unable to leave the facility unaccompanied.

3. Move your parent into a nursing home where skilled care is offered 24/7. Nursing homes have a medical doctor on call and registered nurses on site at all times.

4. Move your parent into a hospice, where end-of-life care is provided by healthcare professionals and volunteers trained to give medical, psychological, and spiritual support to dying patients.

Engaging in crucial conversations with your parent enables a medical plan to be put in place, so everyone in the family can mentally prepare for the "what ifs" that are bound to happen if the parent lives longer, but is not necessarily in good health. When you know various kinds of LTC are available to assist the primary caregiver in following the parent's wishes and making important decisions, this allows all family members to have more balance in their lives.

Be aware that you cannot "toss" your parent into long-term care and expect the facility to do all the work of caring for your parent for you. Your family must continue to be involved on a frequent basis. An assisted-living facility may help your parent in matters such as preparing meals, doing laundry, supervising the taking of medications, and providing transportation to a doctor or a dentist. The more services are used, the higher the price tag is likely to be. In many facilities, residents make a monthly payment based on calculating each service individually. Assisted living is not "free," as some people think it is. In fact, it is extremely costly.

You can keep itemized costs down by participating in many ways just as you would were your parent living with you. By divvying up different tasks between siblings, the workload is lightened and care remains a family affair. For emotional reasons, the entire family needs to make visits to see the parent in the facility on a regular basis, and—if possible—to take the parent out. By no means is long-term care a substitute for participating in the life of your family.

The primary caregiver needs to remain closely involved in monitoring the quality of the long-term care and the charges being assigned to the parent's account, especially as the level of care the parent is receiving deepens. Though my dad had medical insurance, he did not have long-term care insurance. Our failure to plan adequately for the realities of his LTC needs would factor into many of the circumstances and decisions I faced as his caregiver during the next several years. When I first placed my father in an assisted-living residence, my out-of-pocket expenses for his monthly rent started at $2,500 a month. As his needs increased, my out-of-pocket expenses rose to $6,500 a month. This was not government housing, and the housing expenses I'm describing did not include any of the medical charges.

When choosing any care facility, whether it is an assisted-living residence or a nursing home, there are some very important questions to ask.

Key Questions to Ask When Choosing a Care Facility

The majority of healthcare institutions are for-profit businesses, and some are managed better than others. You should interview the staff of several long-term care facilities and take a tour before making your selection. At the admissions office, ask:

- How long has the facility been in business? Use this question to start a discussion of the facility's history and experience.

- How often has the facility changed ownership within the past five years? If there has been more than one owner within a five-year period, ask why.

- What is the likelihood that ownership will change again in the next two to three years? The facility where my father lived for five years changed hands once a year the entire time he was a resident. If I had known this would happen we might have chosen a different facility.

- If ownership changes hands, are the admissions protocols (for example, protocols that allow or forbid the acceptance of residents diagnosed with dementia or another illness) and rental agreements being proposed to us protected from change? New management could very well impose a rent increase. In the case of my dad, I had to continually fight to keep his charges down. At one point, his rent was increased every six months. Don't think that the rent you originally agree to will stay at that amount for a year; it could increase monthly or every six months. One new management wanted to evict residents with dementia. Before they could evict Dad, we changed his diagnosis on his paperwork from "dementia" to "motor-cognitive disability" and he was permitted to stay.

- Does the facility ever change the intake protocol for its residents in order to justify a rent increase? When a facility only bills you from month to month, this entitles the facility to increase your rent whenever it wants and nickel-and-dime you into financial hardship.

- What is the turnover rate among staff members? Your parents need to feel they are in a stable environment. Unhappy staff leads to unhappy residents. If there is a high rate of turnover, this is a place you do not want your parent to live. Run, run, run!

- Are there any licensed nurses or nurse practitioners on staff? How many hours of the day are they available? Nurse practitioners, who are RNs with additional training, are allowed to administer and—in some states—even prescribe medications. Certified medical assistants, by contrast, can only hand a resident a pill and watch him or her swallow it. If there are no nurses or nurse practitioners on staff and only assistants, you will need to develop a "Plan B" in the event your parent ever needs medical care when the licensed nurse is not available.

- How are the sundowner's patients cared for? Sundowner's syndrome is the name for a phenomenon experienced by many people with dementia where their moods change during the late afternoon or early evening hours. Sundowners can become irritable and confused. Often they experience sleep disorders like insomnia or early rising.

- Are the residents allowed to wander around during the night? If so, what does the facility offer these patients to do during the night? If your parent is sleeping, you want to ensure that he or she is not disturbed by others. If your parent sometimes wanders, you want to ensure that he or she is peaceful and has attention.

- How many staff members are working between 9:00 P.M. and 6:00 A.M.?

- How many staff workers are on duty at night between 5 P.M. and 9 P.M.? Who helps the residents get ready for bed, and how long does this process take?

- How often does a physician visit the residents? In assisted-living facilities it is typical for a licensed medical physician to visit once a month or on an on-call basis. In a nursing home, a licensed medical doctor must be on the premises 24/7.

- What is the charge for dispensing medication? Is the charge made by the pill, by the dose, or is it included in the overall monthly rent? Make sure you understand what you are paying for before you sign any papers. Aim to get an all-inclusive rate for rent plus the distribution of medication. Personally, I would never pay a per-pill charge. In assisted living your parent is likely to be given medications by a certified nurse assistant (CNA) who merely oversees the process.

- Are there any extra or hidden charges, such as charges for room cleaning and laundry? How often will there be a rate increase and what is the usual percentage? Remember, this is a business, they will charge for everything possible.

- What is the meal plan? Can the facility accommodate special dietary needs? If your parent has a special diet you must ensure the facility can accommodate it.

- What are the activities, exercise programs, and daily routines? You do not want your parent to live in a place where everyone in sitting around in wheelchairs, staring at the walls. If you see this, run, run, run. Choose a facility where scheduled activities are conducted on a daily basis. Your parent must stay active if physically able to.

- Are any religious activities provided? If not, ask if there are churches or temples in the area that could come and visit, or offer religious services at the facility.

- How often does laundry get done? Who is held responsible for lost or stolen items? Pilferage in care facilities tends to be high. Keep your parents' valuables at home with you. Label all personal items with your parent's name and document each item on a list, having the facility sign the list for the record. By doing so, you'll cut down on theft.

- Does the facility offer personal care, such as hair, nail, and beauty treatments? Many facilities do offer this service at an additional cost.

- What activities are offered, such as bingo, card games, jigsaw puzzles, board games, movies, dancing, aerobics, parties, and excursions? This is very important for your parent's mental and physical well-being. I recommend that you get involved. Volunteer for as many activities as you possibly can. When you are involved, your parent is more likely to get involved, too.

- How would you compare your facility to other similar care facilities? Before asking this question, visit at least five potential facilities in your area. Do your research. Visit SNAPforSeniors.com and read the ratings and reviews. Ask questions of other adult children who have parents residing in the facility. Contact your state licensing department and ask questions about citations, awards, or anything that can help you make the best decision possible. By asking this question, you can sense if they are truthful.

- How many times has this facility been charged by the state licensing division for misconduct? What was the specific misconduct or violation cited? How has it been remedied? Know the answer before you ask the question. Do your homework!

- What are your visiting hours? Can I come and visit my parent whenever I like or only during special hours? If there are posted visiting hours, run, run, run. Posting hours allows staff members to put on a good show. Everything may be great during those hours. But what happens to the parent in between? You want to be able to visit your parent 24/7. It is best to look for a facility where you can visit any time day or night. In this case you will always be able to see what is going on and the staff will not have anything to hide.

You need to feel comfortable with the answers you receive. Much depends on the physical and mental needs of your elderly parent, which are likely to change and increase over time. According to The Aging, Demographics, and Memory Study reported in *Epidemiology* (November 29, 2007), the prevalence of dementia in people over the age of seventy-one and older is just under 14 percent. The odds of developing age-related dementia increase with age, going up to a prevalence of 37 percent in individuals over the age of ninety.

If your parent is moving into a facility while he or she is in good health, you can be supportive of his or her decision-making process by helping evaluate the facility. If you are a family caregiver making a decision about a facility on behalf of your parent, you are responsible for the choice. Conversations about care facilities are crucial because the choice will have a great impact on your parent's quality of life—and yours: a medical, emotional, and financial impact.

The reason I place emphasis on such questions is because of my own personal experience. In Dad's early years in assisted living I didn't know to ask these types of questions. And, boy, did I pay heavily for my lack of knowledge! After I moved him into what I believed was a pristine senior country club environment, the facility was sold at least five times. Turnover in staff came weekly, and protocols for residents changed as every new management came on board. My dad's medication needs never changed. When I signed the admissions forms—meaning, I was basically signing my life savings away—and paid a $1,500 application fee and his first month's rent, I was told to supply medicine and they would ensure he took these medications on schedule while watching him swallow the pills. This service was included in the monthly rent. Six months later, I had to fight the facility in order to stop them from charging us $100 per pill just to watch my dad take his meds. Often facilities will do everything under the sun to get you to pay them more money the longer your parent lives there. Keep in mind, they will also promise you the world and try to make you feel at ease. You must watch everything they do and don't do.

Caregiving Doesn't End When Your Parent Enters a Care Facility

My father remained in the same assisted-living residence for five years. He had a small apartment and was free to come and go as he liked, but staff was on hand to provide his meals, clean his living space, do his laundry, and see that he took his pills. I visited him every day while he lived there, and continued to include him in all of my social activities just as I had when he lived in my house with me. In 2003, I got married. My husband, Orlando, was an electrical engineer. He got along great with my dad, and he, too, was happy to include my dad in our social life. Being in a two-income family eased the financial burden on me of paying for my dad's care considerably.

As my father's primary caregiver, I made the decision to keep my demanding job in the pharmaceutical industry while caring for him so I would be able to afford his care. Although I felt as if the world were slowly caving in around me, I also felt I could balance my career and my caregiving. I constantly prayed to God, asking, "Please give me the strength and knowledge to care for my father in the best possible way and help to heal him and make him whole again." I only wanted my father to have the best, so I was willing to work hard to be able to provide him with private assisted-living care and private physician care whenever the VA Hospital was too busy to see him promptly.

In 2006, I got an alarming call from the care residence in the wee hours of the morning. Dad had been banging his head against the wall, complaining, "There's something in my head!" The facility called an ambulance that rushed Dad to a hospital where he was diagnosed with hydrocephalus, meaning cerebrospinal fluid was leaking inside his skull and causing painful swelling. During surgery, a shunt was inserted in his head to relieve the pressure.

After my dad was discharged from the hospital, I wanted to place him back in the same assisted-living facility where he had been residing, however the duty nurse refused to accept him. They did not want to provide the extra care that my dad required, even though I had stated I would hire an outside medical professional to assist in my dad's rehabilitation. In 2007, for reasons that had nothing to do with my dad, Orlando and I divorced. My dad's care and his financial burdens now rested on my shoulders again.

Keep in mind that medicine and senior living centers in this country are run as businesses! Later I reported the care facility to the State of California, which found my complaint to be substantiated. The facility was cited for not giving us a thirty-day notice before evicting my dad.

A fat lot of good that citation did me! Due to the assisted-living facility's decision, I was faced with the stress of locating an alternate rehabilitation facility for my dad immediately following his emergency surgery. Fortunately, the rehabilitation center of a major hospital was willing to admit him and he was able to remain there for about two weeks in recovery. Unfortunately, late on a Monday afternoon, two weeks after his admittance, I received a call from the hospital and was informed, "Your father is going to be released within a couple of hours." I wasn't given a choice about his release. I believe the hospital's concern was in turning his bed over to the next patient.

My father's imminent release was not due to an improvement in his condition, but because he persisted in removing an IV that had been placed in his arm so he could receive antibiotics. Because of a post-surgical infection he developed, this intravenous medication was intended to help prevent him from contracting a Staph infection, which is common in hospitals.

I asked the hospital to please give me some time to find a place for my father to rehabilitate, and shared with the hospital advice nurse that my father had been evicted from his assisted-living residence due to his new level of care. They pointed me toward a few options, after also threatening to begin charging me $2,000 a day for his room if I didn't pick him up by midnight. Apparently, Medicare would only pay for my father's care if the IV was being administered at the hospital. Since my dad kept taking the line out, Medicare would no longer pay and the hospital was not obligated to keep him. This, of course, placed me in a very difficult situation.

This is how I learned the important lesson that an emergency can be extremely stressful when there is no plan for catastrophic coverage and long-term care. Long-term care facilities can easily take advantage of desperate family caregivers. In our situation, the new private facility I found for my father's rehabilitation requested a $2,000 application fee and $4,000 first month's rent, totaling $6,000, payment due in cash that evening upon his 11 P.M. arrival. I paid it. I didn't feel I had another option, as the rehab center in the hospital was kicking Dad out.

My dad stayed in the new facility for only six months. A higher level of care was being provided there than in his previous residence; it was basically a nursing home. The floor he lived on was a locked-down ward for people with dementia. There was a registered nurse on duty at all times, and a physician was always on call. Every day I went to visit he seemed to have a new problem. One day I went and found dad was not walking, so I had to purchase a wheelchair. He needed to be in an environment like that. But frankly, I was unhappy with the care he was receiving. They made me promises I didn't feel they kept. More importantly, Dad didn't like it there because he believed one of the nurses was mistreating him. When he said that, whether or not it was true, and whether or not the issue could have been remedied, I didn't argue with him. I brought him home again. I renovated the section of my house where he would stay, knocking out a wall so he could have a walk-in bathroom. And I moved dad back in.

3

EMERGENCIES, LIFE-OR-DEATH DECISIONS, AND HOSPICE CARE

AFTER BRINGING MY FATHER HOME FROM THE assisted-living facility, caring for him required more from me on every level, as his condition had worsened. First off, I knew I had to change my demanding work schedule. As a clinical education manager for a drug company, I'd been traveling throughout the country on a weekly basis. This schedule was not a good fit for the increasing level of attention my father needed. I was able to stay in the pharmaceutical industry by switching career tracks. I began to work locally as a sales representative, which cut out nearly all my travel. Each day I'd go on my sales calls and come straight home afterwards. I hired two women to help me, who were my angels. Paris would come and clean Dad's bedroom and bathroom. Melissa would stay home with Dad while I was out. Either she would feed him dinner or I would. Dad was mobile, although he used a cane for walking. Most days he went to the senior center for part of the day. I took care of him on my own between 9 P.M. and 7 A.M.

Mentally, Dad was slipping. Caregivers have to learn to go along with whatever is happening in the mind of a loved one with dementia. You have to relate to them where they are. That's the only way you can survive it. If Dad was singing, I would sing with him. Whatever he enjoyed doing, we did it together. Caregiving of this degree is no joke. You can't do it for money; you have to do it for love, otherwise the effort will kill you. Dad also had sundowner's syndrome. His moods often changed late in the day and his sleeping patterns were wildly different than mine. At 3 A.M. he could be wide awake, fully dressed, and pacing the floors ready to go out. So before going to sleep at night I took to placing a crowbar under the handle of the door to the garage that was adjacent to his bedroom, as a doorstopper, to prevent him from leaving the house and wandering.

The beginning of the end for keeping Dad in my home came when he attacked me one night in the middle of the night. We were alone in the house and he was experiencing a severe episode of sundowner's. He apparently never got to sleep that night. I woke up when he started knocking on my door and shouting. Opening the door partway, I saw him standing outside my bedroom holding the crowbar/doorstopper above his head. He was in his underwear. My eyes bugged out. He kept loudly repeating in an angry voice, "Where is that bastard? I'm going to kill him!"

I knew at once that Dad was in some kind of a trance state. His eyes weren't moving. His skin seemed darkened. I'm not sure why, but I'd guess his blood pressure had spiked, causing his face to flush. He was looking for someone he thought was in the house. He wasn't looking for me. Nonetheless, I was frozen with fear for a minute. I acted then, but only because I knew if

I didn't act he was either going to hurt himself or me, because he was caught up in a delusion. I opened the door and eased my hands up to the crowbar.

We tussled for a few minutes while I tried to get the crowbar out of his hands. It seemed like an hour. His strength was uncanny. Back and forth around my bedroom we went, until we finally ended up in the closet. After I pried the crowbar away from Dad something snapped in his mind. He suddenly stopped resisting, turned away, and walked out of my room. I was terrified and shaking, and my legs were trembling. When I followed him into his own bedroom I found him sitting quietly on his bed. At that point, I was able to get him under the covers and put him to sleep.

The next morning, bright and early, I called the VA hotline to inform them of what had happened during the night. They told me to take Dad to the ER at the VA Hospital in Tracy, California, so the doctors could check his condition. He was in bed asleep. I was a bit afraid to approach him because I didn't know what scenario I was walking into, so I tapped him gently on his shoulder. Feeling this, he opened his eyes and said, "Good morning. How are you today?" He clearly didn't remember the incident.

I replied, "Dad, you had a little problem this morning, so we have to go to the hospital." He was worried he'd hurt or upset me. I reassured him, "I'm not hurt, and I'm not angry with you. We just need to have you evaluated so this doesn't happen again."

If you're a caregiver and anything like this incident ever happens to you, please understand and accept in your heart that it's the disease that is angry with you, rather than your parent.

I drove Dad to the ER in Tracy, where a doctor saw him. He sent us to the San Joaquin Behavioral Health Evaluation Center where they would hold Dad overnight in order to adjust his medication. That night it took six male nurses to calm him down before bed. It's mind-boggling, but when seniors are in delusional states they seem to have the strength of King Kong. With the revised medication schedule things seemed to get a bit better. A few days later, Dad was released from the health center. I moved him to a residence that offered a higher level of assisted living at the cost of $6,500 a month. His care needs had increased beyond my scope and ability to take care of him in my home, as well as my concern for both of our safety.

While visiting Dad a few weeks later, I noticed something else was wrong. I suspected my father might have had a stroke because he was walking with an uneven gait and staggering around the house. He also began needing diapers. I packed him into the car and took him to the office of his primary care physician. After spending the next week visiting various doctors and having lab tests done, all of the reports came out "normal." The doctor then ordered a CT scan to ensure there wasn't a problem with the shunt, or tubing, which had been placed in his head a year earlier to manage his hydrocephalus. I took the order to the adjacent hospital and it was done right away.

There is no waiting period involved in getting the results from a CT scan. As we checked out, the receptionist handed me a copy of the DVD of the brain scan and told me someone would phone me to explain the results. It felt just like a normal doctor's visit day.

Two hours after my father had the CT scan, we were back in the car and on our way to another scheduled appointment. Unexpectedly, I received a call on my cell phone from my father's primary care physician. He asked me where I was, which I thought was a strange question. I told him we were on the freeway. That's when I received the most devastating news anyone could possibly hear. "Your father's life is in danger," the doctor said. "Go to the nearest ER right away," he urged me. "He needs the shunt pulled out. He has hemorrhaging in his brain."

My emotions began running fast. I couldn't believe what my ears had heard. It felt like a bizarre nightmare. It didn't seem real. The only thing I knew was that I had to save my father's life. Fortunately I had my years of knowledge from the pharmaceutical industry to rely upon. "Where is the best trauma center I can take him?" I asked.

He said, "Take him to Trauma in Walnut Creek." I told Dad was what going on and then we high-tailed it twenty miles over to the place he recommended.

I checked Dad into the trauma center, still in denial, thinking, *He can be fixed.* After rushing him there, he was now in the hands of the ER. I handed the on-call neurosurgeon the copy of my father's CT scan, which I'd received two hours prior. My father's report had already been faxed over. The neurosurgeon reviewed the report and saw from the scan that my father was having a massive subdural hematoma, bleeding inside his skull that was putting pressure on his brain.

He pulled me aside, out of my dad's earshot, looked me straight in the eyes, and in a serious tone said, "You have a choice to make. He definitely needs surgery to stop the bleeding. We can either pull the shunt or leave it in place. If you choose to do nothing and we leave the shunt in place, he will be dead within twenty-four hours. The shunt is causing the bleeding, but at the same time it's controlling his hydrocephalus. If we pull it, there is a high likelihood he will end up in a 'vegetative state.' Which would you prefer us to do?"

Wow! When a caregiver is faced with a life-or-death decision, the pressure is overwhelming. My heart was pounding so hard I felt as if it were going to pop out of my chest. I remember asking the surgeon if there was anything else they could do for my father besides the two terrible choices he had given me. It was a Catch-22 situation. Neither of the options he gave me was good, as both had potentially devastating outcomes.

There were only a few hours in which to make this critical decision. As I weighed the options, I remembered the past conversations I'd had with my father regarding end-of-life issues. We had put a medical directive in place for Dad covering things like a 'do not resuscitate' order and the removal of life support. However, we'd never discussed a situation like this one, so I was unprepared for this sudden and unexpected emergency. At that moment, I wished my father had written a medical directive that included greater detail. Then the decision would have been made in advance by my father in writing, and I wouldn't have felt the enormous pressure of making this life-or-death decision for him. I began praying for guidance and contemplating the options.

I wished my father and I had a conversation about what might go wrong with his shunt. But how many of us actually think ahead of time about having a massive hematoma? I never would have imagined that taking my father for a simple doctor's visit could turn into an emergency. That day, September 19, 2008, was the worst day of my life.

One thing that helped me immensely in that moment, and gave me a measure of comfort, was that two nights earlier at the dinner table Dad had said something that touched me deeply. He'd turned to me and said, "Carolyn, I want to thank you. You've done a great job taking care of me. I am ready to go home." Being that he was a pastor, I understood that he meant he was ready to die and be with God.

Hours later, I responded to the neurosurgeon's question of what medical course to take. I told the doctor, "I cannot play the role of God, so I will not make a decision for my father that leads to his death. Therefore I'm asking you to remove the shunt and save his life." I went on to explain, "My father is a child of God. When God is ready to take him home to Glory, then that is when my father will leave the Earth and not before. His life is in God's hands."

The surgery was scheduled for the morning. As we waited, I phoned my brothers and sisters to let them know what was going on. I felt that was important. As Dad was lying on the gurney, just before he went into the operating room, he asked, "Where is Orlando? I haven't seen him for a long time." I phoned my ex-husband and told him what was happening, and then put the phone up to Dad's ear. Orlando told him, "I love you. I know you'll do fine in your surgery."

Dad was in surgery for several hours. I waited in nervous anticipation in the waiting room for news of how it went, praying and pacing, and phoning a few dear friends for emotional support. When the surgeon came out, he told me, "Your father's on his way to recovery now." The surgery had been a success. Dad would live.

Crucial Conversations about What to Do in a Medical Emergency

When you are told by a physician that you have to make a life-or-death decision, in most cases this decision has to be made in a hurry. This was the case with my father's surgery to remove his shunt. As a caregiver, you may have to guess what your parent's wishes would be under a set of circumstances that couldn't have been anticipated. These are times when emotions usually run high. It can feel like a heavy responsibility to make a decision in an emergency situation; however, it is much easier to make difficult decisions if you've had conversations ahead of time. The reason your parent will have chosen you as his or her caregiver is exactly so that you will have the authority to make the best call you are capable of if there is a catastrophe.

Why wait to get your paperwork in order? We'll talk about advance medical directives or living wills, and healthcare proxy or power of attorney in Chapter 6, "Crucial Legal Conversations." Detailed discussions you and your parent may wish to have about possible emergency scenarios may include decisions about:

- Life support of different kinds.
- Resuscitation, if the heart stops beating.
- Palliative care, steps that should or should not be taken to relieve pain and prevent suffering.
- Food and hydration, if these are supplied by medical means, such as tubing.

Your crucial conversations may also need to cover the kinds of emotional, psychological, and spiritual support your parent would wish to receive in a time of crisis or prior to death. When your parent is diagnosed with having a terminal disease or imminent death, there is another option besides nursing home or hospital care that you and your parent may prefer.

Hospice Care for the End of Life

Hospice is a philosophy of palliative care for the incurably ill, much as is given to those who are dying in nursing homes and hospitals, but with the option of dying at home in their own bed. The majority of hospice care is provided in homes. There are also specialized hospice residences where people may go, which have home-like furnishings. Some nursing homes, assisted-living facilities, veterans' facilities, and hospitals offer hospice care in addition to traditional medical care. Dying has physical, emotional, psychological, and social dimensions, and the intent of hospice care is to ensure that people do not die in isolation, as well as that they receive comfort. Over a million people and their families in America choose the option of hospice every year. Most hospices are run as non-profits. They are staffed both by medical professionals—mainly nurses—and trained volunteers. Medicare and most private insurance plans cover it.

A key concept in hospice is the *five stages of coping with dying* model (also known as the five stages of grief) developed by Elisabeth Kübler-Ross. Kübler-Ross interviewed over 500 dying patients in researching her 1969 book, *On Death and Dying*, and discovered that they shared a constellation of responses, which included denial, anger, bargaining, depression, and acceptance. These are not chronological, as dying is not a linear process. Every person's response to severe or terminal illness and death is unique.

Her work has been influential in the way we understand what dying people and their families go through. We'll talk more about the five stages in Chapter 4, "Crucial Emotional Conversations."

I spoke with Patricia Tyson, a hospice nurse in Chicago, about hospice. Nursing was her second career. As she underwent her clinical training, she rotated through different departments in a hospital and recognized that she wasn't attracted to the medical environment. But then she was assigned to a home healthcare rotation and spent one day in a hospice, tagging along with a hospice nurse, which enabled her to see that this was where she belonged. In her words, "Hospice takes us back to the time when people did not go to the hospital to die. They came home to die where they were surrounded by their friends and family, their loved ones. They died in their own home, in bed. People in those days kept a vigil around the sick."

Patricia described her perceptions about the differences between death at home or hospice, and death in a hospital. "The hospital is always focused on a cure, even when they know that a cure can no longer be effective. They feel that until, and even after, the dying person takes the last breath they should continue making efforts. They're practicing medicine. Of course, sometimes they try to pause when the patient's dignity is no longer maintained. But hospital care of dying patients can be like a constant violation.

"I tried many times to run away from hospice, but it's a calling. My calling to hospice is about relationships, not about religion, though I have prayed with families. To work in hospice you have to have what I call the 'hospice heart.' You can't do it as *just care;* this is a political job. You have to like people. You have to recognize the psychological and social aspect of the family dynamics, and you have to be resourceful. You have to be a quick thinker. Hospice is not about giving up on patients; it is about ensuring their quality of life."

Denial of death or the possibility of death—meaning, the response, "This isn't happening to me or to my loved one"—is one of the main reasons grown children and their aging parents fail to have the crucial conversations they need to have, in order to make clear decisions well in advance of sudden medical emergencies. But why wait when so much is at stake?

In the next chapter, we'll begin our exploration of the crucial conversations you and your aging parents, and you and your siblings, would benefit from having as early as possible.

4

CRUCIAL EMOTIONAL CONVERSATIONS

YOU ARE READING THIS BOOK BECAUSE YOU ARE concerned about the needs of an aging parent.

The next three chapters of *Why Wait?* are designed to guide you through a series of crucial conversations with your aging parent (or parents), and with your siblings, so that you and your family will be well prepared for your parent's end-of-life physical, mental, and emotional challenges and ultimate death. If you've read this far, I'm sure we can agree that families need to have these types of conversations early and often, so that medical, financial, and legal decisions can be made appropriately—with clarity and sensitivity—when the need arises, and so the bases that need to be covered are covered. We'll start here by covering conversations that pertain to emotions—but also, first, how to engage in effective conversations within your family.

Because families are social and psychological systems, crucial conversations may become emotionally charged. Nonetheless, they need to happen one-on-one with your parent, as well as in conjunction with your siblings. Siblings also need to be able to communicate well with one another. It is best to begin talking, to resolve relationship conflicts from the past or present, and to make decisions when your parent is healthy and has a sharp mind, so that should an illness, an accident, or another type of emergency occur, you can focus on those acute sudden needs and your relationship. However, a conversation may be even more necessary if you've waited and your parent is ailing. When death comes, proper planning and calm, rational, purposeful, honest, well-intentioned conversations can lessen or prevent family conflict.

How to Engage in Effective Conversations

Relationships can be complicated. One of the greatest skills we need to learn in order to manage their complexity is communication. Business leaders purposefully study communication, as do mediators, counselors, and politicians, because they understand that communication is essential for maintaining harmony, managing hurt feelings, resolving disagreements, coming to a consensus, and steering groups to achieve common goals. This is as much an art as a skill. Some people are naturally gifted as communicators and negotiators, but most of us have to work at it. Learning how to talk to your loved ones—a foundational element of healthy relationships—is not taught in most of our homes. We learn to do it better only with practice, or through specific training—and sometimes, when the going gets especially rough, with the help of mediation.

In his book *Powerful Conversations* (McGraw-Hill, 1999), Phil Harkins defines a powerful conversation as one that advances an agenda, where participants share learning and strengthen their relationship. He believes the most important aspect underlying strong relationships is trust, which can be fostered during and after significant conversations by what he terms the "four Cs": caring, commitment, clarity, and consistency. *Caring,* he asserts, pays dividends. In a conversation, caring is demonstrated by respecting everyone's point of view and taking them seriously. *Commitment* is demonstrated by the promises we make and how we then bring those promises to life in our subsequent actions. *Clarity* means we leave our conversations with clear agreements—we cannot be vague. Finally, we must be *consistent.* Arbitrary or impulsive statements and actions that show we're not caring, committed, or clear, can erode trust.

His recommendation for how to hold a powerful conversation is to:

1. *Plan an agenda for the conversation.* For you and your siblings, this could be to discuss your parent's (or parents') health, or how to support the primary caregiver. For you and your parent(s), this could be to determine their end-of-life wishes, finances, insurance policies, or legal documents, or to check on their health and well-being.

2. *Anticipate the other person's agenda.* When speaking with a sibling, you might, for instance, try to anticipate what's going on in his or her relationship with your parent that is different than what is going on in yours, because this might be his or her priority. Your parent may have a compelling need he or she wants to discuss at the first opportunity—or an entirely different view of what should happen than your agenda allows for.

3. *Identify where your agenda and the other person's agenda meet or overlap.* For family members there are many aspects of life that overlap, although some do not. Knowing where you and your siblings and parent(s) have the same or similar concerns gives you common ground and a sense of mutual purpose.

4. *Think of factors that could throw you off track.* Every family has points of disagreement where tensions can erupt. Even good, well-meaning people can disagree—this is only human nature. So you could believe one course of action is the best for your parent(s), and your siblings or parent(s) might disagree. Your agenda for a conversation could be sabotaged by sibling rivalry, a clash of personalities, unresolved hurt feelings, or something going on in the other person's life—from substance abuse or financial woes and worries, to the gradual onset of dementia and denial.

5. *Choose the right time to hold the conversation.* If you catch your siblings or your parent(s) off-guard by attempting to hold a significant, highly emotional, or uncomfortable conversation when they are unprepared for it, or when they are in the midst of a busy workday or stressed out, chances are your desire to advance your agenda will backfire on you. Sometimes opportunities for crucial conversations arise spontaneously and you just have to seize the moment to say, "What if…?" But usually scheduling a good time for everyone involved to talk is better. Then no one will feel sandbagged or ill-prepared, and everyone can remain relatively calm and focused.

My belief is that crucial conversations should be held face-to-face whenever humanly possible. This way your genuine caring and concern can be displayed by your body language, as well as through your tone of voice and the choice of words you use to express yourself. Of course, families often live at great distances, so a telephone call may be your only option. With modern computerized phone systems, you can set up video calls and bridge lines where more than two people can get on the call simultaneously—and even see each other. If everyone is comfortable with this form of connection it can work well. Just remember that an elderly parent might need help in setting that kind of system up, as older people are less familiar with such technology than younger people are. Of course, you might need assistance, too!

Email communication is absolutely the worst way to communicate important ideas, because email readers supply their own emotional content to the messages they receive. There is no tone of voice, no body language to reply upon to know how the email writer intended a message to sound. If there is any possibility of disagreement, be aware that email messages frequently have been known to exacerbate, rather than reduce, tension and conflicts.

Listening—actively—during a crucial conversation is imperative. A crucial conversation is not the time to be multitasking. You should also do your best to avoid cross-talking and interruptions. Furthermore, a crucial conversation is not the time for game-playing, sarcasm, eye rolling, yelling, silent withdrawal, self-righteousness, or personal attacks. There needs to be a high degree of safety for all of the participants in a crucial conversation, as people can become anxious or confused by the topic of conversation. As a parent ages, suffers illness, or dies, every member of your family from your parent on down will be going through a major transition of his or her own. A wide range of feelings is normal for a grown child whose parent is changing and dying, so please have some compassion for yourself and for your siblings. This is tough stuff. Mutual respect, understanding, compassion, and active listening can defuse a lot of conflict.

Psychologist Marshall Rosenberg, in *Nonviolent Communication* (PuddleDancer Press, 2003), offers his readers steps for honest and empathetic communication. The foundation of his technique is to connect with feelings and unmet needs—both yours and the other person's. He points out that we feel things because of our own thoughts, *not because other people make us.* People may stimulate our feelings, but our judgments and responses to their stimulation are the real cause of what we feel. If we embrace this insight, and take responsibility for what is happening within us subjectively, it can lead to a more compassionate style of conversation.

Rosenberg says that if we listen for the feelings and needs of someone talking to us, we can have empathy for the person. Feelings and needs are universal. We all know what sadness, happiness, and anger feel like. We all know what the needs for sleep, food, and connection—or space—feel like. He suggests trying to imagine with a sense of curiosity how the other person is *feeling* as we listen, and then from time to time to reflect this back. "It sounds like you may be feeling…," "Wow, that must feel very…," "From what you are saying, I am imagining that you could feel…" After the other person acknowledges you got it right, you can go on to make guesses about what this feeling means that the person *needs*.

We don't always know exactly what we need, which is why we often get stuck in a certain pattern of thought and feeling. Having someone actively listen to us with reflections and making guesses about our needs can be very helpful to us to name our feelings and unmet needs.

A universal need that people have is to be heard and seen. By allowing someone else to speak to us for as long as necessary to get a point across, we are giving that person a gift. It helps the person to meet the need for acknowledgment and self-expression. Rather than ascribing our own interpretation to someone else's actions—meaning, trying to be a mind reader—listening with empathy helps us to gain new clarity about what is really going on for someone else.

Notice what is happening within you as you listen. For instance, you may be making judgments and criticisms. You might become angry. If you're angry, stop and breathe. Identify your thoughts. Connect with your own unmet needs. Then express yourself. Once you have heard the other person out, take your turn to describe your own feelings and needs. If you spoke first, then give the other person the benefit of the same courtesy of listening in return.

In caregiving an elderly parent or in forming agreements and a plan of action with your siblings, again, be careful of how requests are made. Remember, there is a difference between a request and a demand. The response to a request could be either yes or no. The response to a demand can only be submission or rebellion. If the speaker lays a guilt-trip on you in the form of a judgment or criticism when you say no to a supposed request, you know a demand was being made. If the speaker expresses empathy for your needs when you say no, you know it was a request. Nobody loves being met by demand after demand. Do your best to go easy and be tolerant.

According to the co-authors of *Crucial Conversations* (Mc-Graw-Hill, 2002), we have to take full responsibility for our own positions. We need to know what we really want to accomplish, and then assess whether our behavior shows that we really want this. We must ask: "If this was what I really wanted, how would I go about getting it?" Especially among siblings, it is easy to fall back into the behavior of adolescence. We tend to regress in the context of the family. But remember there doesn't have to be winning and losing; there can be winning and winning, both honesty and peace. It's very important for family members to make it safe for one another to express feelings and needs without fear of reprisals.

If your family is dysfunctional and you feel it is dangerous to be authentic with your parent or siblings, pay careful attention to when you're starting to feel unsafe. Your cues could be physical, emotional, or behavioral. Crucial conversations can often be stressful. Apologize when necessary. If you blow it or blow up, admit it. Let your family know you'll try to do better in the future. Start over. If you feel you are being misunderstood, find new words to express yourself.

The co-authors of *Crucial Conversations* recommend the following four-question process for making decisions and setting up clear agreements about future actions. Answering these questions could work wonders if you're committed to working together as a team with your siblings and parent.

1. Who?

2. Does what?

3. By when?

4. How will you follow up?

With these sets of guidelines and insights on how to hold effective conversations in mind, let's now look at some of the types of conversations about emotions your family may have.

Emotional Conversations with Your Siblings

Early on, as your parent ages, but while they are still in relatively good health, you and your siblings might check in with one another periodically to see if anyone has noticed the parent slowing down mentally or physically, and open a door to future discussions. You could talk about your individual feelings about your parent's aging process. You could discuss the roles each of you has played in your family since childhood and see if these need updating. The baby sister everyone used to take care of might now be a super-high-achieving adult. The middle child everyone thought was confident and independent might be in need of support.

As time goes by, the child in your family who is named as the parent's caregiver is really going to need support from the rest of the siblings. If you're still engaged in sibling rivalry, you might feel resentful that the caregiver was chosen for this role instead of you, perceiving it as favoritism. If you're a caregiver who has been taking care of a parent on your own for a while and another sibling wants to become more involved, you could feel more entitled to your parent's attention or feel envious about the new relationship between your parent and sibling. Try as best as you can to stay present with the concrete realities that must be managed.

Power struggles about how your parent has assigned the legal authority to manage his or her money or make medical decisions on his or her behalf, and disputes about issues of inheritance can cause rifts within a family. You may need to bring in outside professionals, counselors, social workers, psychologists, or even mediators to help you resolve feelings and disputes. Do not allow your parent's final days and quality of life to become a battleground.

The elderly mother of one primary caregiver I spoke with lived with her daughter and two grandsons for the last nine years of her life, ultimately passing away peacefully in her own bed at age eighty-five with family around her. Although the woman had dementia, her decline was slow and she contributed to the life of the family by doing simple household chores, such as feeding the dog, folding laundry, and putting clothes away. The end of her life had great dignity and she only received hospice care during the last three weeks of her life. Her daughter, Lynn, who was her caregiver, did her best to involve her two brothers. In her words, "I kept them updated even though it was awkward at times to talk about Mom's physical needs in that way. We made decisions together, and felt very fortunate that we could be on the same page. We would talk through how best to handle issues that came up. We would consult with the doctor when necessary, but kept doctor's visits to a minimum.

"Each day, week, or month a part of Mom would fade away, and we would naturally grieve over this as we went along, so that in itself was exhausting. We tried to be aware of our health and needs as well as hers. Yet we always considered what was best for her. I did find that each of us dealt differently with our own feelings over the thought of life without her. We each had our own way of managing our feelings and thoughts. We knew we needed to accept each other's process and not criticize. The grieving process was as individual as we are."

Emotional Conversations with Your Parent

As a grown child, you may currently have a wonderful, loving relationship with your parent, or you may have a strained and challenging relationship with your parent. You may be close or distant on an emotional level. You also may live near or far from your parent. These factors are increasingly relevant as your parent ages, and as soon as caregiving becomes necessary.

Early on, when your parent is still healthy, is a good time to clean up any emotional issues that may have driven a wedge between you in the past. Aging can turn the tables on the parent-child relationship. Where your parent once took care of you, you now may need to step in and take care of your parent. Lingering resentments and unmet needs from childhood and adolescence can cloud your thinking when a reversal of dependency takes place. Maybe you always longed for your parent's approval. Maybe you always felt dominated or ignored. Maybe you didn't understand your parent's choices in life. As an adult, at some point you will have to accept responsibility for giving yourself approval and acknowledgment, standing up for your own interests, and to ask your parent questions if you want answers. Waiting too long means those answers may never be forthcoming. Family history, medical history, lifestyle history, career history, social legacy, and spiritual legacy can all be lost due to dementia or death.

Often, a parent has moved on to live with a second family after a divorce. Absence can lead to unfamiliarity with a parent. Exclusion from a new family can lead to estrangement. Hurt feelings and confusion can fester. If you wait to have conversations to clean up the mess of your unresolved feelings and overcome distance in your relationship with a parent, at the end of life you could miss the opportunity. This is what happened to my friend William.

William was an only child of two only children. Growing up, he had no siblings and no cousins. After his parents divorced when he was a teen, his father moved away and remarried a woman with children of her own. As an adult, he wasn't close with his father. He didn't hate or resent his dad. In fact, he really hungered for his approval. Their parent-child relationship was strained because of living far away, and because William believed his father didn't like some of his choices. Yet William wasn't ready to discuss or renew their relationship. When his father got sick with diabetes, his step-siblings phoned to let him know. But, as he told me, "I didn't know the nature of the illness or understand the severity of the illness.

"When you say someone's sick, if a person is older you just think they're sick: They've got the flu or they've got gout, or they have another issue. To hear that someone had diabetes…well, people can live for twenty, thirty, or forty years with diabetes. That doesn't mean they're going to die immediately, or die within six months, or even six years, of complications related to diabetes." He thought he had time to go see his father and reconnect. It turned out he didn't. His father died before he could visit. Though his father was cared for at the end of his life, William was not his caregiver. He never got the chance to go and tell his dad, "I love you."

Some adult children feel they have amends to make to their aging parents for their own past behavior. One gentleman with whom I spoke had begun abusing narcotics and alcohol in his early twenties. A raging addict for twenty years, he got sober in his forties. In his late-fifties, he went to his parents and apologized, and he asked for forgiveness. His mother forgave him. His father did not. This act of completion made it possible for him to move on with his life. After his father's death, he voluntarily became his mother's caregiver for several years, helping her out financially and also residing with her in her home where he could care for her physically. Later, his mother went to live with his sister in another state, where she passed away.

As your parent ages, you may enjoy interviewing your parent and writing a short book or videotaping them to establish a record for yourself and your siblings, as well as for future generations of children in your family. Doing an oral history project with a parent is a way to honor the parent and spend time together that can pay huge emotional dividends for both of you.

Now, finding out information about your parent and your ancestry may be your main concern from the emotional perspective of the younger generation. But I believe, as an adult, you should begin thinking from the emotional perspective of the older generation. What are your parent's emotional needs? My dad's depression was one of the clues that led me to recognize he required support. At a certain point it's a good idea to monitor the emotions of your parent.

Depression in the Elderly

Depression among the elderly is a serious problem. Often they become depressed because of a variety of physical and social factors. These include isolation, chronic or terminal illness, lack of mobility and/or productivity, decreased independence, memory loss, financial concerns, the loss of friends who have moved or died, or the loss of a spouse. Depression is a cognitive and biological condition that can be treated with psychotherapy and antidepressant medication.

If you believe your parent may be depressed, ask them the following questions taken from the National Institute of Mental Health website. Do you feel:

- Nervous?
- Empty?
- Worthless?
- That you don't enjoy things you used to?
- Restless?
- Irritable?
- Unloved?
- That life isn't worth living?

Also pay attention to whether or not your parent is:

- Sleeping more or less than usual.
- Eating more or less than usual.

According to the National Institute of Mental Health, "For many older adults, especially those in good physical health, combining psychotherapy with antidepressant medication appears to provide the most benefit. A study showed that about 80 percent of older adults with depression recovered with this kind of combined treatment, and had lower recurrence rates than with psychotherapy or medication alone."

It's important to talk with your parent's doctor to assess your parent's condition if you ever see signs that may signal depression, as these could also be signs of other illnesses. The doctor can steer you toward the right experts and solutions.

The Five Stages of Dying and Grief

A parent who is dying is likely to experience depression as well as other mental and emotional responses to this news. So are you. Grief is a natural healing process related to a serious loss or the prospect of a loss. It can seem unbearably painful when we're going through it. But it is a process, meaning that, with time and support, we can move through it and, at our own pace, reach acceptance. Elisabeth Kübler-Ross' five-stage model has been embraced by the hospice movement, physicians, nurses, and therapists, as it is helpful to have an explanation for the conflicting emotions those grieving the loss of their own lives, or the loss of their loved ones, often feel. Knowing these are normal, though extreme, can be a relief.

The stages are as follows:

1. *Denial.* At first, when we're grieving or find out we're dying, we typically deny the news or the loss. "This isn't happening." "I feel fine." "He looks well." "She was just at my house." It's a temporary defense. In this stage, we often withdraw from social activity. Our sense of what is being left behind or lost is heightened.

2. *Anger.* We may become furious at ourselves, at our loved ones, at the doctors, at God, or at the world at large, for letting this take place—even though nothing could be done to prevent it. "Why me? It's not fair." "How dare you let this happen!" "Who is to blame?" Anger usually comes after denial when it is realized that the denial cannot continue.

3. *Bargaining.* In this stage, we negotiate with God or the universe. "If I do *this,* will you stop me from dying?"

"If I do *this*, will you save my loved one?" *This* could be anything from changing a diet, to stopping drinking, visiting alternative healers, following the doctor's instructions to the letter, praying on our knees for hours, and more. "Just let me live to see my grandchildren graduate." "I will give away my life savings to a worthy cause if you change this reality."

4. *Depression.* Here we are numb. Although we may still have anger and sorrow, it's buried. Our energy is so low we feel sluggish and unable to function normally. "I'm going to die, so why bother doing anything?" "I'm so sad that I can't see the point of trying." "Why fight it?"

5. *Acceptance.* When the feelings of anger and sadness taper off, we ultimately accept reality. In this stage, a dying person becomes peaceful, and so do we if we are mourning. "It's going to be okay." "I can't fight it, so I may as well prepare for it."

Remember, the five stages are not set in stone. Some people never reach acceptance. Other people jump swiftly to acceptance. Most people rotate through, or vacillate, between different stages. Emotions can be jumbled and chaotic. Do not try to rush yourself or anyone else through the process of grieving. Asking someone to suppress the truth of his or her feelings is a form of denial.

When you are grieving or your parent is grieving, be aware that good self-care habits reduce the stress of grief. Eating a balanced diet, drinking sufficient non-alcoholic fluids, getting exercise, and resting can help you or your parent cope with your pain and shock until reality can be accepted.

Grief counselors and grief support groups can be enormously helpful, both for those who are dying and those who are left behind. Having social support from your siblings, your spouse, or other people going through a similar experience as yours can help you to be more resilient. Having a chance to express your feelings out loud and process them intellectually with a trusted listener has been shown to reduce stress. See Chapter 7 for more details on self-care.

As the end of your parent's life nears, spiritual support can be incredibly important. Most hospitals and hospices have chaplains who can come and spend time with your parent and you, offering your family solace and guidance in your time of need. You do not need to be a regular churchgoer or practice a specific faith to request spiritual support. Spirit is universal. Counselors and volunteers who work with the dying are trained to honor the unique spiritual needs of individuals.

In the next chapter, we'll talk about preparing financially for the end of your parent's life. If you can eliminate or at least reduce the worry of how to pay for the medical care your parent needs in the final years of life and when death is at hand, your emotional load will be lighter. You will also have more and better access to different kinds of care.

5

CRUCIAL FINANCIAL CONVERSATIONS

MONEY CAN BE A STICKY SUBJECT. PEOPLE HAVE different feelings about money. Some are open about their finances. Others feel ashamed about the condition of their finances. Some think it's rude to talk about money. When it comes to planning for the future needs of an aging parent, however, conversations about how to pay for housing, medicine, and care are crucial. The costs of care at the end of life can grow to be massive. Without insurance and a plan for how your family intends to handle different contingencies, you could be setting yourself up for problems down the road.

One of the first things we did when my dad moved in with me was to review his assets and his insurance coverage. For years he'd been living off modest savings and a small monthly stipend from social security. Although he was also entitled to receive a monthly benefit from the Veterans Administration, he hadn't yet applied for it. The income from the sale of his house was his chief financial asset. As a veteran, he was entitled to receive medical care from the VA.

As a senior citizen, he was entitled to receive coverage from Medicare. I was not able to put his name on the policy for the private pay medical insurance I received as an employee of my company.

Dad and I took some steps together that we believed were appropriate. He filed for the VA benefit. He set up a durable power of attorney for me, which we filed with the VA. I also named him as a dependent of my household on my income taxes so I could take a deduction. (A lot of caregivers don't realize this is allowed.) What we failed to do was buy a long-term care insurance policy for Dad, which would have covered the prospect of assisted living or a nursing home. We figured he'd be able to live with me until the end of his life. We also didn't file Dad's power of attorney with the State of California. We thought filing it with the VA, which is part of the federal government, was sufficient. We didn't know that federal and state agencies don't always talk to one another very well or even agree. This gray area in the law is extremely problematic for veterans and their long-term family caregivers, especially if other members of the family enter into a dispute with the parent's caregiver, as mine later did with me.

For several years, the medical and financial situation in our household was manageable. I was bringing in a good income from my job as a clinical education manager. I owned my house. So Dad didn't need to spend a dime on housing. Although his routine medical needs were growing, those were covered by seeing physicians at the VA Hospital, and the VA covered most of the charges for his numerous medications.

If a branded medication was recommended by a physician, I myself would pay for it, at full price, to assure my dad had the medication. Doctor visits outside the VA were often covered by Medicare (as long as the physician was willing to take it). We paid his Medicare co-payments out of his checking account, which I began to supervise. However, neither the VA nor Medicare covered Dad's dental care or items such as a hearing aid, which are quite expensive. One hearing aid costs as much as $2,000.

It's a good idea for an aging parent to appoint a responsible child as a fiduciary and co-signer on accounts the parent holds with banks and financial institutions, in the event there is ever an emergency or the onset of dementia. We'll talk about how to set this up in the next chapter, "Crucial Legal Conversations."

After Dad moved into an assisted-living facility, I succeeded in paying for his private room through a combination of his social security benefits, his VA benefits, and cash out of my pocket. His housing and care in the residence was a steep expense, but I was glad to contribute to it because I felt it was the right thing for him. This was a contingency for which a long-term care insurance policy would have been a good idea. When Dad had surgery to put a shunt into his head, his insurance covered it because the hydrocephalus was a medical emergency. But the expenses of his care increased while he was receiving rehabilitative care.

When Dad moved back into my home, I paid out of pocket for renovations to his living space, and for the wages of the home care helpers I hired to cook, clean, and spend time in the house with Dad when I was out and working. We never reached the point where he received in-home nursing care, which can be expensive for families who decide to go that route. Once I changed jobs, and became a local sales rep, my income was reduced by half. Thankfully I owned the house and thankfully Dad had his benefits and could go to the VA for medical care, otherwise my finances might have been stretched beyond manageability.

Right after Dad's surgery in 2008 to remove the shunt, my siblings took me to court to challenge my role as my dad's primary caregiver. I'll give you some details about this tragedy in the next chapter. Here, I'll just say that though Dad survived the operation, because he would never be the same cognitively afterwards he was placed in a nursing home. Nursing homes are very expensive. Without properly planning for this contingency, the strain it puts on a parent's financial resources can literally bankrupt the parent. Most elders in our society eventually cash out everything they own at the end of their lives if they do not die quickly. There are protections in place in our governmental systems to look after the elderly, but if you want a menu of better options for your aging parent, you need to develop awareness of what these are.

Where should you and your family begin the crucial conversations about finances?

Crucial Conversations about Money

A major problem is that many aging parents are unaware of the value of their assets, including their investments, stocks and bonds, land, property, 401(k) plans, living trusts, life insurance plans, disability insurance plans, social security benefits, veterans benefits, retirement plan benefits, and the like. In addition, unanticipated issues can come up, such as when an aging parent has a memory disability, and unintentionally forgets where his or her assets are located. While your parent is healthy, it is best to sit down, have a family meeting, and honestly discuss the complete picture of their financial resources.

That being said, all of your parent's assets could easily be wiped out with just a one-month stay in a hospital if they were paying for it exclusively through private insurance.

If you are a caregiver, you should also figure out the value of your own assets. While you are not legally liable for your parent's expenses, you may need or want to dip into them, as I did, when the situation calls for it. Furthermore, you need to ensure that you, as well as your parent, are covered by insurance. As a caregiver, when something happens to you, it puts your parent at risk. .

Here's a true story of what could happen if you or your parent aren't fully covered: My friend William broke his ankle as he was in the final stages of a divorce. He found out that his ex-wife had terminated his medical insurance when he arrived at the ER seeking treatment. He says, "Thank God I had some cash on me and was able to pay for the visit out of my pocket."

Sadly, that same day his mother ended up being admitted to hospital needing surgery for stomach cancer. Her complaint began as a suspicion of a stomach ulcer and then was diagnosed as a more extreme condition. Her insurance didn't cover the full expense of what she needed done. As her caregiver, he says, "It was quite a ride, not being able to drive, not being able to get around because I was on crutches, and not having the money for the $28,000 surgery—and then my mom was in the hospital needing care. After surgery, she couldn't get around." As you can see, when you are a caregiver your parent is dependent on you. This relationship is no joke.

How much does elder care cost? The following estimates will give you a rough idea.

Occasional care. While your parent continues to live independently, your parent may begin to need periodic assistance with lawn care, transportation, and grocery shopping. The cost varies according to the task and according to the town or city where your parent lives. You might be able to find a teenager who wants some extra cash to help out doing chores. If you work with a service, the least you can expect to pay is minimum wage (right now, $7.25 per hour), and in some cases much more. I advise you to shop around for the best solution near you.

In-home care. It is a blessing for a parent to be able to stay at home throughout the end of his or her life. At some point, this can only be managed with assistance. According to the U.S. Department of Health and Human Services, the average cost of having a non-medical care provider come into the home is $29 per hour. But costs vary. Nursing care is more expensive.

Assisted living. Residences that offer an independent lifestyle, yet have trained personnel on the premises to attend to some of your parent's needs, cost an average of $36,372 per year, according to the 2010 MetLife National Survey of Nursing Home and Assisted-Living Costs.

Nursing homes. The same MetLife survey (see above) found that in a residence for elders who cannot care for themselves, or have significant issues that require them to receive round-the-clock care, the average annual cost of a semi-private room is $69,715, while the average annual cost of a private room is $77,380.

No doubt all of these costs will rise every year. Remember, the greater your parent's medical needs, the greater the additional expenses. Those should be considered, too. Furthermore, when considering where to place your parent, remember you may have travel expenses, such as for a car, fuel, plane, or a hotel, to pay whenever you visit your parent. You must factor these into your calculations of how much things cost.

As your parent transitions from being independent to requiring assistance, if you need help in locating housing for your elderly parent, the National Family Caregiver Association has created an online resource called SNAP for Seniors to help you search (SNAPforSeniors.com). This is a current, comprehensive, and objective guide to all licensed senior housing in the United States. For comparable nursing home information, you can also search online through Medicare's Nursing Home Compare (Medicare. gov), which is listed in their resources locator.

Insurance Coverage

One of the crucial conversations you and your parent need to have is a conversation about insurance. At some point, your parent may need short-term assisted or nursing care, long-term assisted or nursing care, home care, or hospital care. As long as your parent is healthy, a managed care insurance plan may be sufficient for his or her needs. Managed care health plans have different models and procedures. They can be Preferred Physician Organizations (PPO), where you can choose the doctors you prefer, including specialists; or Health Maintenance Organizations (HMO), where you see the doctor on duty or a gatekeeper doctor, who authorizes the specialists you can see. Insurance companies like Blue Cross, Blue Shield, Aetna, Oxford, Cigna, and others, may offer both PPO and HMO services.

Examples of the benefits of properly selected managed care plans include: optimized hospitalization, access to branded drugs versus generic drugs, and determining co-pay versus out-of-pocket expenses. In some cases, generic drugs are fine, they do the job; in other cases, the brand-name drug is preferable.

You must choose a healthcare plan that would be the most beneficial, the most impactful, and the most supportive for the needs of all of your family members, including your parent. Study and scrutinize the plans you consider before buying. Consider the future as well as the present. As people age, they often need to see specialized physicians and healthcare providers, such as neurologists, cardiologists, podiatrists, physical therapists, and ophthalmologists, among others. As your parent ages, having the ability to choose the specialists that are best for his or her healthcare needs may be the better option. In many cases, a higher cost plan may be more beneficial and more positive in the long run than a less expensive plan.

In the United States, individuals aged sixty-five and older are entitled by federal law to receive Medicare benefits. You need to be aware, however, that Medicare benefits are limited. One problem with relying upon Medicare alone is that many physicians do not accept Medicare insurance in their private practices. Another problem is that Medicare does not pay for many medical services your parent may want, nor will it pay for certain drugs your parent may need.

In some states, Medicare has an ambulance charge limit of once per year; meaning, a second ambulance ride would have to be paid for out of pocket. And, in most cases, there is a co-payment due for services partially paid for through the Medicare system. Therefore, if your parent does not have access to cash or another type of medical coverage, your family needs to discuss who will pay for the overflow of charges.

There are many types and categories of Medicare, making it complicated for patients and for those who render services to patients, such as doctors and hospitals, to understand what services are applicable. There have been cases where hospitals discharged patients prematurely because their Medicare coverage had reached its maximum. Medicare limits the benefits it pays for hospitalization care and routine medical coverage, and it does not pay for assisted living. After death, Medicare also does not cover funeral expenses. Funeral expenses can add to the financial burden on your family, if you do not plan ahead of time for how to manage them.

Medicaid is a federally supported and state-funded program intended for the very poor. Each state has its own Medicaid plan for its residents. Many health institutions won't accept Medicaid, meaning that, in practice, being covered by Medicaid is nearly the same as having no insurance. On Medicaid, the options for health services, hospital care, and medications are very limited. Medicaid patients are only given generic drugs. Coverage does not pay for assisted living.

There are two considerations when your family is having a crucial conversation about your parent's insurance coverage. First, there is the consideration about having the right coverage in place and how to handle co-payments and gaps in coverage. Second, there is the consideration of who pays the insurance premiums. A grown child who is a caregiver may want to step in at some point and pick up this expense, in order to protect the parent and the family from financial turbulence in the future. If other siblings understand that the primary caregiver is going to incur expenses related to the care of the parent—everything from food, clothing, medicine, and insurance premiums, to a reduction in income from lost wages, if the caregiver has to modify his or her work habits to stay at home with the parent or drive the parent to the doctor—then the caregiver's siblings might consider making a contribution to the caregiver for these expenses.

Perhaps the biggest secret in the pharmaceutical industry is that companies have dedicated patient assistance programs. If your parent cannot afford the medication he or she needs, you can phone the company and ask to be connected to the patient assistance program, or visit the company online (just search the name of the company along with the phrase "patient assistance program"), and you can read about the rules to apply for this on their websites. These programs cover everything from cancer medications, to high blood pressure medications, and so on.

It's not good to stick your head in the sand like an ostrich trying to hide. Bring money issues out in the open where your family can discuss them. This is much healthier. Speak with a financial adviser or a professional bookkeeper if you and your siblings need help straightening out and updating your parent's financial records or federal and state taxes, or just need advice about future planning. See the Recommended Resources section for additional guidance.

When it comes to managing money or insurance, one child in a family may be more skillful than another. When your family agrees to work as a team, try to ensure that the right person for the job is put in place as your parent's financial representative. The caregiver is likely to need regular access to the parent's accounts; however, another sibling can help the caregiver with this responsibility if money and recordkeeping is not the primary caregiver's strength. Every family is unique. But I can assure you that money is one of the main issues that can tear a family apart. Probate courts are filled with families arguing over who has control of a parent's assets before and after death. Greed and a sense of entitlement are the sources of most of these conflicts.

In the next chapter, you'll learn how a parent, by filing just a few legal documents, can set a plan in motion that will protect the family as a whole when it comes to matters of money.

6

CRUCIAL LEGAL CONVERSATIONS

OFTEN ELDERLY PEOPLE HAVE DIFFICULTY describing what they want to occur at the end of their lives. The subject is uncomfortable. It can stir up fearsome images and feelings of grief. Nonetheless, one of the most important things we can do for those we love who are advancing in years or are terminally ill, is to initiate conversations with them to help them clarify their wishes and make formal decisions. Remember, there are ways to have these conversations that are gentle, respectful, and helpful, rather than pushy. After talking things over with your parent and giving him or her a chance to reflect, these decisions should be set down on paper in signed legal documents that will protect your parent, and ensure his or her personal choices are honored by doctors, hospitals, family members, and the courts.

Requesting that your parent document his or her end-of-life wishes and decisions about care, finances, and inheritance is an important preventive measure that benefits not only your parent, but also the rest of your family. The purpose of taking this step is to prevent lawsuits and avoid the heartache and tragedy that are the byproduct of conflict at the end of life and following death.

My question, as always, is: Why wait? Have the crucial conversations, do the paperwork, and then you and your family members can go back to the routine of living your best lives, secure in the knowledge that affairs are in order.

Three main documents need to be prepared.

1. *An advance medical directive, also known as a healthcare directive, a living will, or a healthcare proxy.* This is a set of instructions given by your parent specifying what types of actions should be taken for his or her health in the event that he or she is no longer able to make decisions due to illness or incapacity. For instance, a medical directive lets your parent specify his or her decisions about artificial life support in advance. This ensures not only that your parent's wishes will be honored, but it also protects your family from having to make these difficult, deeply personal choices yourselves.

2. *A durable power of attorney.* With this document, your parent can appoint a trusted person, like a long-term caregiver, to manage important financial and legal matters on his or her behalf. Your parent can choose to have the power of attorney take effect immediately or to go into effect only in the event of illness, unconsciousness, or another kind of incapacitation.

3. *A last will and testament.* With this document your parent names the person or people he or she wants to manage his or her estate, and it provides for the transfer of his or her property after death. Without a will in place (the legal term is "dying intestate"), the courts will decide how to divide your parent's property.

Your parent may also wish to consider creating a fourth document: a *revocable living trust.* Like a will, this document provides for the division of your parent's assets after death (at which point it becomes *irrevocable),* but also during his or her lifetime. It is called "revocable" because the trust allows your parent to change the terms of the settlement of property or revoke them altogether, whenever he or she wants to as long as he or she is alive and competent.

Setting up trusts is becoming more popular, as our elders are living longer and requiring care for longer terms. A trust enables your parent to name his or her caregiver—or another responsible person, like a friend or a banker—as a trustee to manage the property named in the trust, in the event of your parent's incapacitation. A trustee does not necessarily become a beneficiary of the trust. One advantage is some tax benefits a trust confers. Another is that by their nature, trusts do not go through probate administration, which is a definite advantage when an estate is complex. However, a trust should not be considered a substitute for a will! Even when there's a trust in place, your parent still needs both documents.

A fifth document that benefits family members more than a parent is a relatively new type of document. When siblings are not in full accord about the care of their aging parents, a mediator can help them to create *a sibling agreement,* which all parties sign and adhere to from then on. This customized contract can spell out everything from who is promising to do what and how decisions will be made in the future about different tasks and responsibilities, to how to compensate a primary caregiver for expending time and expense, or promises of non-interference by siblings who do not wish to be involved. This type of caregiver agreement prevents conflicts from getting ugly.

Obstacles to Legal Decision-Making

If, for any reason, a family has a mistrust of authority figures, such as lawyers and doctors, accountants and bankers, then just filling out paperwork and getting involved with the legal system and financial institutions can cause feelings of suspicion and mistrust to arise. Anyone who has ever been taken advantage of financially or legally feels this same sense of repulsion to the process of doing the legal paperwork necessary to prepare appropriately for a parent's end of life.

When families have shameful secrets, this can prevent their members from seeking professional help with legal documents. There is a strong desire not to have "dirty" secrets revealed by discussing the family history. Secrets that families typically hide include divorce, physical abuse, sexual abuse, and substance abuse. If families have a group dynamic that revolves around alcohol they may not be entirely functional. If they are struggling with poverty and lack of education, their economic situation could feel like an overwhelming, shameful problem.

Other obstacles you may face in getting the legal decision-making process going could include your parent's reluctance to appear to be "playing favorites" with one child over another, or denial of his or her mortality, or issues related to senility or poor health. Let's discuss these three stumbling blocks for a moment.

First, if your parent knows which child he or she wants to depend on (and/or can depend on) to handle finances and medical decisions at the end of life, but refuses to put the choice in writing, your parent's reluctance to be clear about this preference could backfire and actually end up doing exactly what it's intended to prevent: namely, create sibling rivalry. Arguments can and do frequently erupt in the corridors of hospitals when an aging parent is incapacitated or dying. One child may have been caring for the parent for years and then another child steps in at the very end of the parent's life with entirely different ideas about the quality of care, and types of medical treatments the parent should receive. Hospitals have to adhere to the decisions of whoever holds the documents that assert legal authority.

Second, if your parent is in denial about mortality, he or she is not alone. As I've said before, as a culture we are averse to having conversations about death. We often say we're doing paperwork "just in case something happens," which is not rational, because something is going to happen to everyone: We will die. The only things we don't know are whether our death will be caused by an accident or an illness, and whether it will be sudden or gradual, peaceful or painful.

Third, if an individual is developing senility or has full-blown dementia, he or she may not have the mental capacity that meets the standards under the law to sign legal documents. The law is designed to protect people whose faculties are compromised from being taken advantage of by devious family members who want to control and inherit their assets by altering their instructions.

Contact an elder law attorney for guidance on filing for guardianship if your parent is already having trouble making decisions on his or her own behalf. Typically, these documents are filed in family courts. It's best to work with a specialized elder law attorney at this point so everything can be done in a manner that no one else can challenge—or would want to challenge.

I spoke with Helen, a seventy-year-old woman from Oklahoma City, who was her mother's caregiver for twenty-five years before her mother's death in 2009. Her story shows how bad it can get. Her father was a laborer and her mother a homemaker. They raised ten children: seven girls and two boys. Helen, the third eldest child, says, "They didn't have the kind of education that enabled them to make enough money for all of us and also to save much for retirement, so I stepped in to help my mother after my father died in 1971. After what my parents had done for us, struggling to raise up a family of ten in the worst of times. . . I never gave it a thought."

As her mother began to move into her elder years, part of Helen's support for her was helping her manage her financial affairs. Helen wrote out her mother's checks, and drove her places. Her mother had never learned how to drive. She was a good baker (at times making baked goods to supplement her income) and an avid grocery shopper. Helen took care of her though she was living independently in a senior citizen's home. There, her mother lived in her own tiny apartment.

The family was close knit, although there was rivalry among the ten siblings. One of them would try to out-compete the other. They grew up in that fashion and their rivalry continued into adulthood. In 2005, when her mother turned ninety, Helen began trying to convince her mom to create a trust, and a will, and a health directive. She reminded her mother that the grown siblings were very competitive with each other and it was difficult for them to agree on how to do things. Her aim was to build her mom's understanding that having a will and a trust would prevent them from having to go to court. Her mother was independent and didn't want to think about losing her freedom. It took Helen a year to persuade her it was the right step before they finally got the paperwork done.

Helen's mother wrote a trust and a will and these were nota-rized. It's important to point out that a last will and testament is *confidential;* it's not usually read until the person who wrote it is deceased. Even so, once her mom had done her will, Helen's sib-lings started badgering her mother with questions about it because she had named Helen and Helen's daughter as trustees. It took a couple of years for the controversy in the family to ease up over that issue.

New dissension arose when her mother began needing more support. She started getting forgetful in the kitchen. One time she flooded her downstairs neighbor by leaving a tap run-ning. Another time there was a smoke accident and the walls needed to be repainted. When the senior residence charged for damages, Helen suggested her mother move in with Ann one of her sisters. Helen and her sister, Ann, lived next door to each other. From then on, they cared for their mother's day-to-day physical needs together. Helen continued to manage her mom's finances.

Sometime after the move, a third sister called adult protective services and made an accusation against Ann, saying her home was a bad environment. APS investigated and found this claim groundless. Then a fourth sister, Joyce, who had recently moved home to Oklahoma from another state, started jockeying for con-trol of their now-ninety-six-year-old mother's affairs.

Helen took a vacation. When she got back she discovered Joyce's name had been added to the bank accounts. That was a surprise, since she hadn't been consulted. Joyce had somehow per-suaded her mother to sign power of attorney papers putting her in charge of medical decisions if she became incapacitated.

Helen's mother had probably acceded to Joyce and signed new paperwork because she didn't want her children to argue. Unfortunately, in the process, she'd sealed her own fate. Joyce started running rampant through her mother's life, making all kinds of changes to her routines without consulting Helen, who as you'll recall, had been caring for her mother for over twenty years. Joyce started bringing in a home healthcare aide to put their mom through a variety of exercises. There was nothing wrong with this, in general, except that Helen's mom had been fine and switching her routines was stressful to her.

One day Joyce said she was taking their mother to the grocery store, but instead took her to an appointment she had secretly made at a new clinic where a new doctor gave their mother an echocardiogram—even though she hadn't been having any particular heart trouble. A couple of days later, their mother had a brain hemorrhage. Helen believes the stress of the visit to the doctor was too much for her mother's constitution. As Helen was coming home that day in her car, she saw her mother being lifted into the back of an ambulance to rush her to the hospital.

The heartrending part of Helen's story is that her mother could have been treated for her condition and might possibly have recovered from it, but her sister, Joyce, would not allow the hospital to offer her any meaningful treatment. Joyce told the doctors she held medical guardianship over her mother and instructed them to give her morphine for pain relief, but to withhold food and liquids. Thus, Joyce consigned her mother to die. Helen spent fourteen days by her mother's bedside, watching her waste away as a consequence of her sister's decision.

After her mother's death, Helen's family was further torn apart when some of her siblings challenged their mother's will. They understood perfectly well that their mother didn't have any assets to speak of, yet when Helen went to probate court to file the paperwork in a routine manner seven of them showed up accusing her of fraud. She says the judge got fed up as they spoke out of turn. In her words: "He told them, 'You know, this is my courtroom. Usually I don't let things like this happen here. But I want to advise you all that since you don't understand the law, the library is across the hall from my courtroom. You need to go over there and look up wills. It will tell you exactly how a will is done and probated.'" After that he had Helen raise a hand and swear an oath. Then probate was concluded.

Advance Medical Directives

In preparation of this chapter, I spoke with attorney Carolyn L. Rosenblatt, R.N., attorney, author of *The Boomer's Guide to Aging Parents* (Aging Parents Press, 2009), who prior to practicing law worked as a registered nurse for ten years, a career which, among other things, included service to elderly patients. She has extensive, hands-on experience in elder care, has written several books for family caregivers of aging parents, and works with caregivers on matters of general elder care and financial, insurance, and elder law. One of her areas of specialization is the mediation of conflict between grown siblings. She and her husband, psychologist Mikol S. Davis, Ph.D., co-founded AgingParents.com to be a resource for caregivers.

Rosenblatt says, "When a family finds an elder in a position where that person cannot make any words come out, or they're not conscious, and the person can't say what he or she is looking for, or can't say what his or her wishes will be, then some other people have to make that decision for the elder. That decision can be colored by their own prejudices, their own fears, and their own unwillingness to deal with dying, which is one of the reasons that conflicts between family members can arise. Fistfights and painful arguments are the last thing you need when you've got a relative in the hospital, in the Intensive Care Unit, maybe comatose, and maybe with IVs and machines all hooked up to them. It is not desirable to be standing in the hallway screaming at each other about whether or not to resuscitate that person when/if the time comes.

"When someone is in need is not the time to be determining whether or not to give that person some lifesaving measures. Deciding whether to give or withhold treatment and measures is a big decision. A crisis is a terrible time to be making such decisions. So it is important to do this preparatory paperwork in advance, in a calm and sober moment. This is the only time we have a chance to work up to talking about life-threatening situations, and to come at it slowly if we need to overcome resistance from all parties involved.

"By having these conversations we can find within ourselves what it is we do want at the end of life. My experience is that if you allow people the space to talk about these subjects without pressuring them, and if you give them some support, most people are willing to say, 'I want to die with dignity and I don't want to have a whole lot of stuff done to me,' or whatever else their own choices are.

"We need to start the conversation ourselves. We need to be supportive in the process. And if this is all too much for an elderly person to handle, elder law attorneys are usually quite good at helping people get through filling out the documents that need to be filled out.

"In our state, California, this is a paper we call a *healthcare directive;* they're called similar names in other states. They're usually obtainable free on the Internet. You check off boxes and decide what it is you want, and then sign it. You don't have to have the healthcare directive notarized if you have non-nursing home care people serve as your witnesses. If your elder is in a nursing home, the state ombudsman needs to be there to witness it, too. It's not a big deal."

A medical directive or living will covers the following types of questions:

- Who do I want to make medical decisions for me when I can't? Who do I want to decide about tests, medicine, and surgery?

- Do I want artificial means of support to be used to keep me alive? If a treatment has started who do I give the authority to stop it?

- Do I want to be resuscitated if I die during a medical emergency?

- Who do I give the authority to place me in an assisted-living facility or nursing home?

- Do I consent to be moved to another state if necessary so that my wishes will be carried out?

- Do I want pain medication as I am dying? Do I wish to refuse pain medication?

- Do I wish to donate useable organs or tissues at death?

Many states, although not all fifty of them yet, now recognize a thoughtful and very detailed version of an advance medical directive called "The Five Wishes." You can find a copy of this online at AgingwithDignity.com, with instructions for how to fill it out. What I like about "The Five Wishes" is that it enables the individual whose directive it is to describe how he or she would like to receive comfort, such as by having someone pray with him or her, or hold his or her hand, and what types of pictures and belongings he or she would like to have around the room. It describes what the person wants done with his or her remains. It also lets the person whose directive it is leave messages for loved ones, such as "I want my children to know that I love them."

Durable Powers of Attorney

Money is the issue most likely to tear a family apart—sometimes temporarily, but in many cases for a lifetime. Probate courts in our nation are backed up with cases of families fighting over their entitlements and inheritances, frequently while their parents are still alive. With a durable power of attorney or a revocable living trust, which names a fiduciary, or representative, to manage your parent's money, these types of court cases can be prevented. You can find the forms you need for your parent's state of residence online. See Recommended Resources.

A fiduciary should be selected by your parent for having solid qualifications to manage his or her finances and good motives; meaning, there can be no greed attached to serving your parent in this capacity. The fiduciary must be an excellent record-keeper and accurately track your parent's medical and living expenses, and banking transactions, in an expense ledger where they can be audited.

If you are a primary caregiver, it's important for you to be aware that you could be dragged into a probate court if you are managing your parent's money without a power of attorney, or a trust naming you as the parent's fiduciary. I say this from first-hand experience. After my father's surgery in 2008 to remove his shunt (the tube that was surgically placed in his head to relieve the hydrocephalus), my twin sister dragged me through the courts in several jurisdictions. I do not know her motivations. I believe she was looking for money she thought my father had; but it was never found because it simply did not exist.

Yes, the surgery was a success, because my dad lived. But the doctor had been correct with his warning that my father's mental capacity would never be the same. A couple of days following the surgery, as Dad was recovering in a nursing home, my sister, who had visited him in the hospital, made her first formal accusation against me—an allegation of elder abuse. A temporary restraining order was put in place against me so that the claims could be properly investigated. That was when she also filed a motion without my knowledge, to be made my father's conservator in a state court.

In different filings on different occasions in different jurisdictions, my sister made various claims that I had stolen my father's money, that he was homeless, that I had physically abused him, and that I had falsified his signature on the power of attorney form that he had filed with the Veterans Administration. It absolutely enrages me when I think about it. None of these cases was ever heard by a judge. In a couple of instances, a judge refused to hear the case because he found no grounds for the filing.

A couple of other times my sister and I would be standing before a judge about to hear the case and—right before the actual hearing would start—she would say, without explaining her reasons, "I'm withdrawing the case." She must have known that the minute I presented my evidence she would lose the case and it would go on record. Twice I had my father's doctor appear in court at great expense to testify on my behalf. While I do not know for sure, I can only imagine that she wanted to burden me with expenses.

Investigations must be done when the allegations made are so serious to an elder's well-being and personal safety. If you ever suspect elder abuse or neglect of your parent by someone in a nursing home or by a sibling, I urge you to file one. You may or may not remember, but the Academy Award-nominated actor Mickey Rooney had to get a restraining order at age ninety to protect him from abuse by his fifty-two-year-old stepson, the child of his late wife. Although that case was settled out of court, Rooney's lawyers claimed he had been restrained against his will in his home, bullied and harassed, deprived of food and medication, and that his stepson had confiscated his passport and identity cards. Rooney was lucky to have concerned people looking out for him.

Elder abuse is often linked to money. Rooney made his initial accusation in February 2011. Then, as reported on Wikipedia: "On March 2, 2011, Rooney appeared before a special U.S. Senate committee that was considering legislation to curb elder abuse. Rooney stated he was financially abused by an unnamed family member. On March 27, 2011, all finances of Rooney's were permanently handed over to lawyers over the claim of missing money."

In my opinion, my sister was abusing the court system, and I felt abused by her. Nearly thirteen years before she made her claims, my dad appointed me to serve as his medical and financial fiducia-ry. A VA official affirmed me as I pledged to honor and follow the directive my dad signed, and care for him according to his wishes. At that moment, I felt great pride to have been selected. I under-stood the responsibility was great and I always hoped and prayed Dad would never come to the point of becoming totally disabled.

The two most important things I forgot to do that made me vulnerable to my sister's claims were 1) to secure this document in a safe place in the event I would ever need to prove I was my father's legally appointed fiduciary, and 2) to file the conservator-ship document with the state as well as at the VA. I knew the im-portance of the document, but I took it for granted after a while because I was so well known within the medical and financial institutions where my father and I conducted business. I had no idea there was a gray area in the law between the federal and state authorities. Dad and I had not been aware that we needed to do a power of attorney in both places. We thought one was sufficient. We were wrong. I could have filed for state conservatorship, but I unknowingly failed to do so.

Take it from me: Trying to obtain a copy of legal documenta-tion from the VA takes time. If your parent is a veteran and you are his or her appointed representative, you must file the power of attorney both in the state system and the federal system.

No matter what your parent's military status is—whether or not he or she is a veteran—my urgent recommendation is to *keep your records in a secure place* like a safety deposit box at the bank. Keep a second copy in a fireproof box at home. It is essential to be able to get your hands on all of your important records pertaining to your parent twenty-four hours a day, seven days a week.

The stress of continuously fighting to defend my status as my dad's fiduciary from the legal challenges of my siblings ultimately began eroding my health. It was so stressful that one day, a few months after his surgery, I had a panic attack and checked myself into the hospital overnight. Because of my background in pharmaceuticals, when I realized I was experiencing sensations of tingling in my left arm and shortness of breath I suspected I was having a heart attack. Thank God, I wasn't. There was a period of time when I had continued working even when my foot was broken. That choice had adversely affected my back, which was also giving me trouble. Furthermore I'd neglected my health in different ways that were also catching up with me, including ignoring the symptoms of a growing fibroid tumor that eventually ruptured. I had to have surgery to address that condition.

A dear, dear friend advised me that for my own good I had to stop my efforts. My dad was in a nursing home. Bills were beginning to mount. My siblings were challenging me over his guardianship. I knew my dad would not be kicked out of the nursing home, because the court had mandated that he remain where he was until the case was settled. He was safe. So I reluctantly relinquished my role as his fiduciary. It was a heartbreaking decision, but I had to make it to preserve Dad's well-being and my sanity.

I wish I could tell you that my situation is unusual. But I cannot. Similar conflicts between siblings happen every day and they are affecting the lives of seniors and family caregivers across the country. Accusations fly. The courts get involved. The parent loses. But long-time caregivers also suffer. That is why having conversations and following them up with paperwork is crucial. No one comes out a winner when families fight.

Sibling Contracts

Carolyn Rosenblatt shared the following insights with me. She said: "As a mediator, one of the most frequent issues that come up among family members is the issue of the parent's money. Who is in charge of the money? Who controls the money? What's going to happen to Mom and Dad's money, their things, their home, and so forth? Issues of sibling rivalry and control go on in lots of families. The other component in these situations is the elder's gradual loss of capacity to make safe money decisions. Dementia is so prevalent and such a huge problem, especially for people over the age of eighty-five, that people must deal with it in advance.

"Your chances of developing Alzheimer's disease, the most common form of dementia, are approximately one in two by the time you reach the age of eighty-five. Half of our parents are going to have this problem if they're still alive by that age.

"It could affect half of Baby Boomers in their fifties today if medical science hasn't figured out how to treat it better by then. Dementia is a scary problem because it sneaks up on you very gradually. It can take years for symptoms to truly manifest themselves. When it comes to money decisions, Alzheimer's disease robs us of our best judgment even in the earliest phases of this disease.

"We can start losing our judgment in discerning that someone wants to take advantage of us, or that someone is lying to us, or that somebody's out to get us. Those things are usually pretty clear judgments that we can make when we're younger and savvier. Even if we are affected by Alzheimer's disease or another form of dementia, for a long time we may act as if we're all right. We may be independent. We may be physically capable of caring for ourselves, driving a car, living in our house independently. Yet we can't see trouble coming when someone is starting to manipulate us with regard to our finances.

"The reason I think *caregiver contracts* are important—and contracts between siblings are one kind of caregiver contract—is that they help protect against the possibility that the elder who needs care, or may need care soon, is going to make some foolish decision later on. This eliminates fighting about what's fair.

"Now, let's take a typical example. Let's say we've got a family with three siblings. They're scattered around the country. Mom, who is a widow, lives by herself in her little house and her daughter lives nearby. Because the other two siblings are far away, and because the daughter is a daughter and women tend to be most of the caregivers, the daughter ends up paying more attention to Mom because of her proximity and inclination. The daughter starts helping her mother with the grocery shopping when her mom has some physical ailments. She starts taking Mom to the doctor. As Mom's physical capacities decline further, she starts having memory problems. Now the nearby daughter starts doing more and more, until pretty soon she's quitting her job to take care of Mom full-time because, if she does not, Mom is going to have to go into a nursing home.

"That's a typical situation. There are millions of caregivers like the daughter across this country. This situation developed gradually; maybe it took two or three years during which the nearby daughter assumes that role.

"She's now given up her source of income. And maybe she's divorced and had to give up her apartment, or she's got a husband who's complaining all the time that she's never home. Whatever it is, what's fair is this: It costs money to take care of an elder with ailments—particularly dementia. It costs a lot of money. We can place the elder in a facility (and pay thousands of dollars a month), or we can have a family member do that job (for which we otherwise would be paying those outside people). Even if our elderly relative is in a nursing home we still have to supervise him or her, and we might even have to pay to supplement the care.

"My question to everybody is this: Shouldn't we compensate the caregiver who is a family member—particularly if he or she has had to give up a job? That's what a sibling contract, a caregiver contract, enables to happen. It sets it in writing."

She continued: "I'm a strong advocate for caregivers and promote recognition of both the importance and the difficulty of the job of caregiving. I'm a caregiver, too. I have a disabled brother. He can't do much of anything without some kind of help in terms of money. He's physically able. He can drive a car. He can care for himself. He lives alone. But he doesn't have a credit card. He can't use a computer. He can barely use a cell phone. He would be taken advantage of by other people if I wasn't helping him. He already has been many times. So I took over for him. Now if helping him also involved physical care and he had the money, I would certainly insist that I be paid something for the work of doing that job.

"People are strange about this subject. They discount how difficult a caregiver's job is. They fail to recognize what it would cost to put Mom or Dad somewhere so somebody else could do the caregiver job. And worst of all, when their motivations are about greed, they don't want to spend their aging parent's money on care because they hope to inherit it. That's the truth."

Carolyn made a great point that in mediation issues be-tween siblings can get "unwound much sooner." The goal is to "get to the underlying part of the conflict, which has to do with mistrust, greed, rivalry, competition, and past hurts." Mediators delve into such issues, because, as she says, "If we give voice to those emotions we have a far better chance of resolving conflicts before they become lawsuits. Even when they become lawsuits, we can address them in mediation before they become trials where nobody really wins."

It's important to point out that the contracts called "sibling contracts" are customized to cover the unique situation being ex-perienced by the siblings who are party to the agreement. In addi-tion to compensation, a sibling contract could include points such as: promises of non-interference (I could certainly have used this with my siblings who did not get involved with Dad's care until he was incapacitated), details about actions and division of labor, and more. A sibling contract takes the pressure off sibling caregivers on the "back end" of caregiving, because things have been discussed and spelled out clearly at the "front end."

Last Wills and Testaments

A will is the document indicating how property will be disbursed after death. Your parent is really doing your family a favor by preparing a will, as he or she won't be around to experience its impact personally. You can find services online that can facilitate your parent to prepare a will quickly and easily that is legal in his or her state of residence. You might also help your parent to hire a lawyer who specializes in estate law or elder law. See the Recom-mended Resources section.

If your parent establishes a living trust, your parent is eligible to do a kind of will that is known as a *pour-over will.* According to FreeAdvice.com, "This kind of will 'pours' any property the deceased still owned at the time of death into the trust that the person set up during his or her life."

Some people intentionally choose not to put all their property into their trusts during their lifetimes for reasons related to taxes and property insurance. Other people forget to put newly acquired property into their trusts. They buy a valuable object and simply fail to go back over to the trust to document it properly. A pour-over will automatically includes assets such as these and ensures they are distributed along with everything else according to the wishes of the deceased.

Changing the Laws to Protect Long-term Family Caregivers

Since I took care of my dad for twelve years, I understand first-hand that being an aging parent's primary caregiver is not an easy journey. It can be heartbreaking and emotionally wrenching. Not everyone is called to it. It's like an anointing from God. Even if you have a large family with many siblings, they won't necessarily be willing or able to put out the same effort for your parents at the end of their lives. Some families have problem siblings, siblings who are alcoholics or drug users, or have mental challenges or life circumstances that preclude them from being caregivers. Millions of people across the country, however, are going through the same process. If this is your path, please always remember that you are not alone.

The important thing for you, as a caregiver, is to remember to take care of yourself and also to protect yourself from challenges to your status. Those who are not in the same position as you may not be able to fully understand what you are going through.

I've been lobbying the United States Congress to pass new laws that will protect longstanding family caregivers from the malice of their siblings. My goal is to close the gap I identified between the state and federal authorities, by making it harder for long-time caregivers to be displaced by siblings who have not been involved in the care of their elderly parents. I knocked on doors at Congress and The White House until my congressman agreed to meet me.

My prayers were also answered when I met Ameenah Fuller, publisher of *Looking-In Politics* magazine, who is a former candidate for California State Senate District 31. I literally had said, "Dear God, I need somebody with a political background to help me because this is a huge fight. I cannot do it alone." On cue, she arrived. She's a political activist who holds a master's degree in public policy from New England College and shares my goals. I'm so grateful to have her as an ally in this important cause.

Changes in the law are well overdue and much needed in our society, and I assure you that the fight will continue until our Congress and local legislators make these changes. If you want to help, please write letters to your elected officials. Also visit me on my website, CaregiverStory.com, for more details.

TAKING CARE OF YOURSELF
WHEN YOU ARE A CAREGIVER

AFTER GOING THROUGH THE JOURNEY AND heartache of being the sole family caregiver for my father for twelve years, and then enduring the pain of legal conflicts with my siblings, I ultimately asked myself a key question: What would you do differently if you could do it all over again? My answer was simple: I would take better care of myself at every step in the process.

In looking back, I do not regret my decision to be my father's caregiver. I did it for love. It was rewarding to have the opportunity to give of myself to my father in his time of need, as he gave so much to me. Even so, it was exhausting. It took a very real physical toll on my body.

To be an effective caregiver, you must take care of yourself as well. Now on the other end of caregiving, I find that exercise and meditation help me to relax as I never did beforehand. I wish I would have known to nurture myself better while I was on the journey with my father.

After interviewing over one hundred former caregivers nationwide, it still amazes me that they all gave me similar responses to this one question: What would you do differently? It's exceptionally common for us caregivers to fail to take good care of ourselves. We're so busy caring for our loved ones that we forget how important our own self-care is. As a result, caregivers end up with back and neck problems. We end up with all sorts of different physical ailments. We even end up in the hospital.

When I asked one woman if there was something she'd do differently if she had it to do over again, she too remarked, "I didn't give consideration to my own health and I should have." She'd had so much love for her mother that even though she herself has diabetes and hypertension, when at her mother's bedside in the hospital her eating habits lapsed. Matters came to a head one day when she thought she was having a heart attack. She couldn't make it from her chair in the living room to her dining room table without feeling like she was going to collapse. She went to see the doctor and was told she had severe anemia. She'd run her body down. Like many other caregivers, who somehow manage to keep themselves going with adrenaline in a crisis mode, in the transition period when she was grieving her mom's death the woman fell apart.

Caregivers are notoriously rundown. A common thread in all of my conversations with the caregivers of aging parents I meet across the country is how beaten up they feel. They're trying to help someone they love and falling to pieces in the process. At my company, Grandpa's Dream, we've established a national Caregiver's Appreciation Day to give people a chance to show family caregivers their appreciation. For more details, visit CaregiverStory.com/appreciation.

Here are some of the ways you can take better care of yourself as a caregiver:

Reach Out for Support

While caring for your aging parent, it is critical that you reach out for support for yourself. If you get along well with your siblings, you can support one another in mutual caregiving of your parent by contributing time, energy, and your personal abilities to the process. As the adage goes, many hands make light work. Even in optimal situations like these, however, there is stress.

Many caregivers find themselves in the position of being the only person in a family caring for a sick elderly parent, even when they have siblings. If you are a sole caregiver, there are many reasons why this may be so, ranging from the fact that you live nearer to your parent; to having had a closer relationship with your parent over the years; having the financial means to supply the care that's required; having time available in your schedule to give care; or having siblings who would be inappropriate caregivers due to alcoholism, drug addiction, or temperament.

In addition, many caregivers simply get beaten up emotionally and physically while going through the process of caring for an elderly parent. In that case, the caregiver *must* reach out for the help they need in order to survive this very heartbreaking experience.

While caring for my dad, I simultaneously juggled my career with my role as a wife and as a daughter. My former husband, Orlando, got along great with my dad. He even came to visit him in an assisted-living facility at one point several years after we split up because my father wanted to see him. To make things easier on me, I would take my father to every social event

I was invited to. I decided that if I couldn't take him, I simply would not attend an event.

Sometimes I would phone my siblings just so Dad could hear their voices. I maintained hope that one of them would jump in to help me periodically with the tremendous responsibility of caregiving. When they didn't, I simply placed my life on hold and put my physical and emotional needs after my dad's. I prayed daily, "Dear God, please give me strength."

I did reach out to extended family members, assisted-living communities, my church, and a senior adult day treatment center for support. Day treatment especially was an environment where Dad was socially, mentally, and emotionally stimulated while being around his peers.

As a caregiver, your parent is not the only one who has a health or emotional concern. Your health is also at risk. As a family caregiver, you could be at risk for depression and chronic illness, and a decline in the quality of your life. You are considerably less likely than a non-caregiver to practice preventive healthcare and other self-nurturing behaviors.

According to the Family Caregiver Alliance (see Recommended Resources), "Caregivers report problems attending to their own health and well-being while managing caregiving responsibilities." Issues many caregivers report experiencing include:

- Sleep deprivation.
- Poor eating habits.
- Failure to exercise.
- Failure to stay in bed when ill.

- Postponement of medical appointments or failure to make them in the first place.
- Excessive use of alcohol, tobacco, and medications for depression.

Caregiving an aging parent can be an emotional roller coaster. On the one hand, caring for your family member demonstrates your love and commitment for your parent, and it can be a very rewarding personal experience. On the other hand, exhaustion, worry, inadequate resources, and continuous care demands are enormously stressful. Studies show that an estimated 46 to 59 percent of caregivers are clinically depressed.

Special Concerns of the Working Caregiver

As a caregiver, you may feel your career options are limited. You may not want to take risks. In my case, my father had only me as his provider and no one else, so I worried a lot. *If I lose my job, what type of medical care and housing will my father have?* I felt I had no choice other than to work very hard so that I could provide my father with every possible resource.

In 2007, shortly after my father's first surgery, I broke the fifth metatarsal bone in my foot. This wasn't part of my plans. Although the entire bottom of my foot had turned purple, I asked the orthopedist if he was sure I'd broken my foot because I didn't have "too much" pain. He told me, "You have to take at least six weeks off work and rest for your foot to heal properly."

"Are you kidding me?" I asked. "I could lose my job! You can't be serious." I recall my paranoia. I knew my job security was only as good as my last sales performance, and it was getting close to the end of the fourth quarter. "What can I do to keep working?" I asked. "Can I work with a foot cast?"

The orthopedist pointed out, "You won't be able to drive your car with a cast on your right foot." That was logical.

In denial, I replied, "Oh, I can easily drive with my left foot—no problem." The day he treated me was the only day I took off from work, even though I desperately needed to rest. The doctor placed a cast on my foot that extended all of the way to the base of my knee. I recall walking out of his office that day with a set of crutches at 3:00 P.M. and being back in my sales territory the next morning calling on the physicians who were my clients. Business as usual!

Due to my fear of losing my job, along with the income and insurance that accompanied it, I neglected my own body, health, and well-being. Now many years later, I look back and see how crazy it was that I was willing to work with a severely broken foot, when I could have taken a leave of absence under the full protection of the Family and Medical Leave Act. Some employers do not share information about this federal law with their employees. As a caregiver, however, having knowledge of this act will help you in planning your care strategy for your parents.

Let's look at the stipulations of the act. The following information is taken from Wikipedia.

The Family and Medical Leave Act of 1993 (Wikipedia)

The Family and Medical Leave Act of 1993 (FMLA) is a United States federal law requiring larger employers to provide employees job-protected unpaid leave due to a serious health condition that makes the employee unable to perform his or her job, or to care for a sick family member, or to care for a new child (including by birth, adoption, or foster care). The FMLA is administered by the Wage and Hour Division of the Employment Standards Administration of the United States Department of Labor. The bill was a major part of President Bill Clinton's agenda in his first term. President Clinton signed the bill into law on February 5, 1993 (Pub. L. 103-3; 29 U.S.C. sec. 2601; 29 CFR 825), and it took effect on August 5, 1993, six months later.

Understanding the Family and Medical Leave Act of 1993 (Wikipedia)

On October 28, 2009, the President signed the National Defense Authorization Act for Fiscal Year 2010 (2010 NDAA), Public Law 111–84. Section 565 of the 2010 NDAA amends the military family leave entitlements of the Family and Medical Leave Act (FMLA). These amendments expand coverage for "qualifying exigency" leave to eligible employees with covered family members in the Regular Armed Forces and coverage for "military caregiver leave" to eligible employees who are the spouse, son, daughter, parent, or next of kin of certain veterans with a "serious injury or illness." On December 21, 2009, the President signed the Airline Flight Crew Technical Corrections Act, Public Law 111-119, which modifies the FMLA eligibility requirements for flight crew members. This Fact Sheet does not incorporate these amendments to the FMLA.

The U.S. Department of Labor's Employment Standards Administration, Wage and Hour Division, administers and enforces the Family and Medical Leave Act (FMLA) for all private, state, and local government employees, and some federal employees. Most federal and certain congressional employees are also covered by the law and are subject to the jurisdiction of the U.S. Office of Personnel Management or the Congress.

The FMLA entitles eligible employees to take up to twelve workweeks of unpaid, job-protected leave in a twelve-month period for specified family and medical reasons, or for any "qualifying exigency" arising out of the fact that a covered military member is on active duty, or has been notified of an impending call or order to active duty, in support of a contingency operation. The FMLA also allows eligible employees to take up to twenty-six workweeks of job-protected leave in a "single twelve-month period" to care for a covered service member with a serious injury or illness. See Fact Sheet #28A: The Family and Medical Leave Act Military Family Leave Entitlements.

Employer Coverage

The FMLA applies to all public agencies, including state, local, and federal employers, local education agencies (schools), and private-sector employers who employed fifty or more employees in twenty or more workweeks in the current or preceding calendar year, including joint employers and successors of covered employers.

Employee Eligibility

To be eligible for FMLA benefits, an employee must:
- Work for a covered employer;
- Have worked for the employer for a total of twelve months;
- Have worked at least 1,250 hours over the previous twelve months; and

- Work at a location in the United States or in any territory or possession of the United States where at least fifty employees are employed by the employer within seventy-five miles.

While the twelve months of employment need not be consecutive, employment periods prior to a break in service of seven years or more need not be counted unless the break is occasioned by the employee's fulfillment of his or her National Guard or Reserve military obligation (as protected under the Uniformed Services Employment and Reemployment Rights Act (USERRA), or a written agreement, including a collective bargaining agreement, exists concerning the employer's intention to rehire the employee after the break in service. See "FMLA Special Rules for Returning Reservists."

Leave Entitlement

A covered employer must grant an eligible employee up to a total of twelve workweeks of unpaid leave during any twelve-month period for one or more of the following reasons:

- For the birth and care of a newborn child of the employee;
- For placement with the employee of a son or daughter for adoption or foster care;
- To care for a spouse, son, daughter, or parent with a serious health condition;
- To take medical leave when the employee is unable to work because of a serious health condition; or
- For qualifying exigencies arising out of the fact that the employee's spouse, son, daughter, or parent is on active duty

or call to active duty status as a member of the National Guard or Reserves in support of a contingency operation.

A covered employer also must grant an eligible employee who is a spouse, son, daughter, parent, or next of kin of a current member of the Armed Forces, including a member of the National Guard or Reserves, with a serious injury or illness up to a total of twenty-six workweeks of unpaid leave during a "single twelve-month period" to care for the service member.

Moving Forward

When my journey with my dad was abruptly ended by one of my siblings making false allegations of financial and medical abuse, I recognized I needed emotional help. I searched for a professional therapist who specialized in senior care, caregiver support, and family conflicts. I knew I needed to speak with someone who specialized in this particular area of focus to help me understand exactly what I had gone through, and how best to move forward in my life. I was truly a train wreck and needed to get back on track again, but I didn't know how. I eventually found a fantastic therapist. Her practice was a whopping ninety-mile drive from where I live. After my first visit with her, I felt as if a burden had been lifted. The key question I had for her was, "What could I have done differently in the care of my dad?"

For the longest time, I'd felt that if I had only known the right questions to ask the doctors or suggested another form of treatment, things could have ended differently for my dad. On some level, I began to blame myself for my dad's illness. For months I'd been upset with myself because I'd been unable to save my dad by somehow fixing him and making him the person he once was. Understanding there was nothing else I could have done was one of the biggest hurdles for me to cross. Like many caregivers, I was experiencing grief—which often includes a constellation of anger, denial, and depression, before acceptance and peace can be attained.

Another issue I worked on in my therapy sessions was the dysfunction in my family. I did not understand why my siblings hadn't chosen to help me care for our father, or why they had chosen to attack me by making allegations against me in three different legal jurisdictions.

Through therapy, I began to recognize that the conflicts I experienced with my siblings had nothing to do with Dad's health challenges. They did, however, have to do with past sibling rivalry, abuse, and family dysfunction. Basically, I had been raised as if an only child by my dad, while they'd lived with our mother. Through therapy, I came to believe that the hurt, jealousy, resentment, and pain my siblings must have felt as children were being carried over into their adult lives.

It was clear I had to work actively on forgiveness and love. Over a period of months and years, I was able to face my feelings of resentment, guilt, loss, and anger. After the whole experience in the courts, I felt as if God and my dad had both forsaken me. *Why did I have to go through this type of pain?* I asked. Going to therapy, engaging in conscious acts of forgiveness, and finding my greater purpose in life were the foundation of my healing process.

Yes, I said "healing process." For any course of self-discovery and grieving has alternating phases of progression and regression, good days and bad days, up moods and down moods. Healing for me involved learning new ways of being more self-nurturing.

Now, I am able to enjoy some of the activities I previously enjoyed before my dad got sick. The emotional pain I used to feel when I thought about my situation has been transformed into energy that I use to help others avoid the pitfalls of caregiving when a parent becomes ill.

Get Support

Sadly, caregiving will take a heavy toll on your body, mind, and soul if you don't get adequate support. Being a caregiver involves many stress factors. You will find that the dynamic within your family of origin will change, there will be disruptions in your immediate household, your social life and friendships will get put on hold, there will be new and unanticipated financial demands made on you, and you may experience pressure from your employer when you need to take days off, not to mention the sheer amount of work involved in having a dependent parent whose affairs and well-being you come to manage.

As I mentioned elsewhere, the rewards of caregiving an aging parent who is sick or coming to the end of life are mostly intangible rewards, and often there is no hope for a happy outcome. So finding the support you need to stand up under the pressures of caregiving is essential for your mental, physical, and emotional health, and essential for you to be successful at giving care. It's like the moment when the cabin pressure drops in an airplane and the oxygen masks pop out of the overhead compartment. You have to put on your own mask first before you can help anyone else. Flight attendants remind us of this every time we fly, because it's true: If you can't function because you can't "breathe," for any reason, you will be useless as a caregiver.

Through my experience, I can now look back and see how stress piled up on me while I was going through my caregiver journey without a roadmap. You can avoid the frustration, disparity, and burnout if you have a plan in place. Put yourself in a position to avoid the very real dangers of caregiver burnout by following a few essential guidelines:

- Embrace your feelings. Caregiving can trigger a host of difficult emotions, including anger, fear, resentment, guilt, helplessness, and grief. As long as you don't compromise the well-being of the care receiver in the process, allow yourself to feel whatever you feel.

- Educate yourself as much as possible about your aging parent's condition, so that you won't experience the added strain of not knowing what needs to be done.

- Know your limits and how much you can realistically handle as a caregiver. Don't overexert yourself. If possible, ask your immediate family and extended family for help. Otherwise, seek help in your community, from doctors, and from caregiver support groups.

Respite Care

It's a fact that caregiving is an extremely demanding and difficult job that no one is equipped to do alone. Reaching out and getting the help you need to preserve your mental health and physical well-being is therefore crucial for both you and the parent you are caring for, especially if you live together.

During the time I cared for my dad in my home, I got into the state of mind and a routine of doing it all without taking a break. I did not have support from my immediate family. On several occasions, I asked my siblings to give me "just one day off" and offered to pay their travel expenses and put them up in my home, but they did not come. Although I did try to take a break for a day every now and then, I was never successful in doing so. While caring for my dad, there always seemed to be an emergency. I felt I couldn't leave his side because something might happen to him or he would cause an accident: a fire, a fall, wandering off. I was aware that I could contact a care facility that would take him off my hands for a month so I could have a thirty-day respite from caregiving, but I never felt comfortable leaving Dad with strangers.

In retrospect, I now realize I should have taken time off at least once a month and gone to a day spa, a weekend retreat center, or just stayed home lying in bed without feeling guilty. Every caregiver needs to take a break at intervals from the demands of caregiving.

So let me give you the advice I didn't take myself and wish I had: Consider *respite care*. Respite care offers an excellent opportunity for you to enjoy a short-term break in caregiving to relieve your stress, restore your energy, and improve the balance in your life. It is an especially good option if your situation is like mine was and you're finding it difficult to get support from siblings or friends. There are many respite care options and strategies available.

A good way to start researching your local respite options would be to contact educational and encouraging caregiver support groups in your area. Also use the community resources in your area, such as churches, extended family, friends, and health-care professionals. Don't be afraid to make phone calls, ask for help, and accept the help you need. Whatever you do, please don't wait to reach out until you are already overwhelmed, exhausted, or your health is failing. Reaching out for help sooner will greatly benefit you by preserving your well-being.

Physical Needs

In the period immediately following caregiving, I started getting my life back on track emotionally. I also addressed physical needs I'd neglected during my journey with my dad. Years later, I discovered that working with a broken foot hadn't been the "best thing" I could have done for my health. Not staying off my broken foot as the orthopedic surgeon recommended produced the long-term effect of chronic lower back pain. It's most likely I'll have to deal with this undesirable condition for the rest of my life.

Today, I give myself permission to take care of me. Every morning for an hour, I attend a water aerobics class that helps me to manage my pain, as well as to relax, reflect, meditate, and ultimately rejoice. Yes, I said, "Rejoice"! In this class, as I float and kick my legs, I think of the wonderful lessons on the magnificent glory of God that my dad taught me. I think of the pelican flying to the Moon to drop off one grain of sand and flying back to Earth, repeating the same task until there no longer is any sand on the Earth. Then I think about how Dad and the way he loves me is like that pelican with the grains of sand that never ever finishes his journey. It reassures me and makes me glad when I find myself missing him.

I also often think about how God's love for me is eternal. When I was a child, my dad often told me I was "God's special child" and that God had great things for me to do in my life. I never would have imagined the great work and the calling God has anointed me to do for humanity. However, through all of my years of heartache and pain, I learned to trust in God and, as a Christian, I've tried to walk in Jesus' footsteps. To this day, I feel the presence of my dad's spirit with me always, saying, "Carolyn, I love you. Always take care of yourself."

The way I began taking care of myself was taking a long look in the mirror and asking, "Carolyn, what type of health do you want for yourself, and what would Dad have wanted for you?" I began by taking baby steps to improve my health. After all, I had not derailed and become a train wreck overnight. I understood that getting my health back on track was going to take time as well. I started by going for physical therapy for my back three times a week.

I continued to see a local psychologist for counseling. Through our sessions, my therapist helped me realize the "big picture" of my life and the journey I'd had to go through in order to become who I am today. Being a child of a pastor, God had a mission for me and work for me to learn to do through my horrible experience. Now my life is filled with a mission and purpose to help others, like you, avoid the mistakes my family has made, and change the structures in our society related to the caregiver experience. I learned how to grieve mindfully by avoiding things that would trigger sadness in me, and strive for physical and mental wellness. I learned how to avoid negative outcomes of conflict by actively seeking resolutions for problems.

As an example, I am now actively working with my current U.S. congressman, Jerry McNerney, and with social activist Ameenah Fuller to pass a federal law in Congress that would hold the Office of the Inspector General (OIG), the Veterans Administration, and the judicial system responsible for ensuring that the decisions veterans and senior citizens make about the appointment of legal, financial, and medical fiduciaries are honored in the event of their disability. Most importantly, I hope to see laws put in place to stop the abuse of honorable caregivers by dishonorable family members seeking nothing more than personal gain.

Choosing to seek effective solutions for the problems I faced as a caregiver is perhaps the most important thing I've done to heal my grief and move forward in my life. Taking action to solve those problems has changed my future. Thanks to the awesome support I have received, my attitude is now a more positive one, which is giving me confidence and strength in my abilities to excel in my mission to educate both seniors and caregivers.

Walking in Spirit

Since January 2009, I have not seen my father. The legal battles with my siblings tore me apart so much inside that I had to say goodbye to him. Though he is alive at the time of this writing, he is ill and living in a nursing home. I would love to be with him to hold his hand and hug him, but I cannot if I am to remain well myself. Because of our untimely separation, I've learned to walk in spirit with my dad. No one can prevent us from being together spiritually! My dad still guides me in spirit; I can literally feel his love and his arms around me in every moment of the day. I rarely make any decisions unless I hear both a clear voice from my dad's spirit and the voice of the Lord. I hear his soft voice directing me to do the work of God. It is always clear direction and has never led me down the wrong path.

Dad used to say that when God speaks it is a soft nudge you can feel in your bones. For me, the experience is like suddenly knowing the right answers to a difficult test, answers you couldn't have known. Have you ever been in a situation where you just felt you shouldn't do something and you did it anyway, resulting in an unfavorable outcome? Well, that sensation you ignored very well could have been Spirit talking to you.

Following years of prayer, I now have sensitivity to feeling God's nudges and hearing his directions for me. I have learned to move by faith rather than by sight. This is what "walking in Spirit" means to me. As my dad used to tell me, "Let your conscience be your guide and you will never go wrong, because that is the Holy Spirit talking to you."

If you are seeking spiritual comfort, here are some verses of scripture from the Bible that I've found particularly valuable.

> *"You, my brothers and sisters, were called to be free. But do not use your freedom to indulge the flesh; rather, serve one another humbly in love. For the entire law is fulfilled in keeping this one command: 'Love your neighbor as yourself.' If you bite and devour each other, watch out or you will be destroyed by each other."*
> —Galatians 5:13–15

> *"So I say, walk by the Spirit, and you will not gratify the desires of the flesh. For the flesh desires what is contrary to the Spirit, and the Spirit what is contrary to the flesh. They are in conflict with each other, so that you are not to do whatever you want. But if you are led by the Spirit, you are not under the law."*
> —Galatians 5:16–18

"So I say, walk by the Spirit, and you will not gratify the desires of the flesh. Now faith is being sure of what we hope for and certain of what we do not see."
—Hebrews 11:1

"So we fix our eyes not on what is seen, but on what is unseen. For what is seen is temporary, but what is unseen is eternal."
—2 Corinthians 4:18

"The fruit of the Spirit is love, joy, peace, patience, kindness, goodness, faithfulness."
—Galatians 5:22

WHY WAIT? RESOURCES

Programs and Services to Help Caregivers

To help you find the emotional, medical, financial, and legal resources you need in order to care for your aging parent, I have created the following resources.

Access Free Downloads and Newsletter

Go to CaregiverStory.com to download resources for caregivers of aging parents. While you are there, you may subscribe to our monthly online newsletter, which will keep you updated on new developments.

Access Free Blog—BabyBoomersGuide.org

The Baby Boomers' Guide blog is the hub of ongoing discussions and links to video resources, as well as interviews with family caregivers and professionals who work with the elderly and their caregivers. You are able to post comments and connect with peers all over the world.

Connect via the Social Networks

I welcome connection. Follow me on Twitter @BBBoomers-Guide. Also, please join The Baby Boomers' Guide page on Facebook and the Baby Boomer Caregivers group on LinkedIn. You can contribute and become part of my growing community.

Why Wait? Coaching and Seminars

More detailed assistance in working with the issues of family caregiving for an aging parent is available through Grandpa's Dream LLC. For more information on these services, please visit CaregiverStory.com.

Why Wait? Keynote Presentations

If you are interested in having me give a keynote address to your corporation, association, or professional or nonprofit organization, please contact John W. Sandifer, J.D., Director of Public Affairs for Grandpa's Dream at John@CaregiverStory.com or phone: (510) 304-8092.

RECOMMENDED RESOURCES

The following books, publications, and websites may help you in taking action on the ideas you've been reading about in this book. Although this is by no means a complete list of resources for caregivers of aging parents, I hope these resources will be useful and informative. Additional resources for seniors and caregivers are available on CaregiverStory.com.

BOOKS

The 36-Hour Day: A Family Guide to Caring for People Who Have Alzheimer Disease, Related Dementias, and Memory Loss, 5th edition, by Nancy L. Mace, M.A., and Peter V. Rabins, M.D., M.P.H. (The Johns Hopkins University Press, 2011).

The Boomer's Guide to Aging Parents: The Complete Guide by Carolyn L. Rosenblatt, R.N., B.S.N., P.H.N., Attorney (Aging Parents Press, 2009).

A Bittersweet Season: Caring for Our Aging Parents and Ourselves by Jane Gross (Knopf, 2011).

The Caregiver's Survival Handbook: Caring for Your Aging Parents Without Losing Yourself by Alexis Abramson, Ph.D. (Perigee, 2011).

Crucial Conversations: Tools for Talking When Stakes Are High by Kerry Patterson, Joseph Grenny, Ron McMillan, and Al Switzer (McGraw-Hill, 2002).

Powerful Conversations: How High Impact Leaders Communicate by Phil Harkins (McGraw-Hill, 1999).

Nonviolent Communication: A Language of Life by Marshall B. Rosenberg, Ph.D. (PuddleDancer Press, 2003).

On Death and Dying by Elisabeth Kübler-Ross, M.D. (Scribner, 1969).

They're Your Parents, Too! How Siblings Can Survive Their Parents' Aging Without Driving Each Other Crazy by Francine Russo (Bantam, 2009).

Why Can't We Get Along? Healing Adult Sibling Relationships by Peter Goldenthal, Ph.D. (John Wiley & Sons, 2002).

SENIOR LIVING

American Association of Retired Persons (AARP)

AARP.org

A nonprofit, nonpartisan organization that helps people fifty and over improve the quality of their lives.

American Senior Benefits Association

ASBAOnline.org

ASBA is a not-for-profit organization focused on advocacy and education for men and women age fifty and over.

American Society on Aging

ASAging.org

Developing leadership, knowledge, and skills to address the challenges and opportunities of a diverse aging society.

Eldercare Locator

www.ElderCare.gov

A public service of the U.S. Administration on Aging that connects to services for older adults and their families.

National Council on Aging

NCOA.org

Information and resources aimed to improve the lives of older Americans.

Senior Living Source

seniorlivingsource.org

A directory with a free referral service that can help you reach out to many communities to request free information from them, or even a free consultation.

SNAP for Seniors

www.SNAPforSeniors.com

Senior living and housing information.

U.S. Department of Housing and Urban Development

portal.HUD.gov

To find information on housing options, search "senior housing."

FAMILY CAREGIVING

Aging Parents

AgingParents.com

Information and advice for caregivers of aging parents.

Caregiver Resources from Medicare.gov

Medicare.gov

Search for "Caregiver information center."

Caregiver Resources from Medline Plus

NLM.NIH.gov

Caregivers are people who take care of other adults, often parents or spouses, or children with special medical needs. Some caregivers are family members; others are paid.

Department of Labor—Family and Medical Leave Act

DOL.gov/dol/topic/benefits-leave/fmla.htm

Information about the Family Medical Leave Act (FMLA).

Family Caregiver Alliance

Caregiver.org/caregiver/jsp/home.jsp

A public voice for caregivers, FCA brings information, education, services, research, and advocacy together in one place online.

National Caregivers Library

CaregiversLibrary.org

This site will help you navigate to the most appropriate place to start your search for information and pertinent resources.

National Family Caregiver Support Program
AOA.gov
The National Family Caregiver Support Program (NFCSP), established in 2000, provides grants to states and territories, based on their share of the population aged seventy and over, to fund a range of supports that assist family and informal caregivers to care for their loved ones at home for as long as possible.

Respite Care Locator
ArchRespite.org
Respite is planned or emergency care provided to a child or adult with special needs in order to provide temporary relief to family caregivers who are caring for that child or adult. For more information on the delivery of respite care, click on "The ABCs of Respite."

Caregiver Stress
CaregiverStress.com
A website from Home Instead Senior Care that offers a free Stress-Meter assessment tool to measure your level of stress, and advice about what you could do to manage it better.

Today's Caregiver
Caregiver.com
Find a caregiver support center near you.

HOME CARE

Center of Design for an Aging Society

www.centerofdesign.org

Eldercare at Home

www.HealthinAging.org

A comprehensive online guide for family caregivers.

Medicare Home Health Compare

Medicare.gov/homehealthcompare/search.aspx

Find detailed information about every Medicare-certified home health agency in the country.

Universal Design Resource

UniversalDesignResource.com

A website of resources on universal design, a set of design principles that guide a designer to consider how easily the product or environment can be used for the widest spectrum of users, people of differing ages and abilities.

ASSISTED LIVING AND NURSING HOMES

Care Look Up Provider Database

CareLookUp.com

A database of 115,000 care providers to aid you in finding the right skilled nursing facility or nursing home, elderly care provider, or home healthcare provider.

National Long-term Care Ombudsman Resource Center
ltcombudsman.org

Locate an ombudsman, state agencies, and citizen advocacy groups.

HOSPICE AND PALLIATIVE CARE
The National Hospice and Palliative Care Organization
NHPCO.org

National Hospice Foundation
Nationalhospicefoundation.org

HEALTHCARE, INSURANCE, AND GOVERNMENT BENEFITS
Health Plans of America
HealthPlansAmerica.org

Compare providers, plans, and options.

Health Quote Expert
HealthQuoteExpert.com

Find affordable healthcare.

Hospital Compare—U.S. Department of Health and Human Services
HospitalCompare.hhs.gov

Each hospital's information and measures all in one place.

Medicare and Medicaid Overview
CMS. gov

Medicaid—U.S. Center for Medicare and Medicaid Services
CMS.gov/home/medicaid.asp
Providing Medicaid healthcare.

Medicare—U.S. Center for Medicare and Medicaid Services
CMS.gov/home/medicare.asp
Providing Medicare healthcare.

National Association of County Veterans Service Officers
www.NACVSO.org
Assistance for veterans of the American military.

National Library of Medicine—Medline Plus
NLM.NIH.gov/medlineplus
Find health information for seniors.

National Private Duty Association
PrivateDutyHomecare.org
Find a private duty nurse.

Patient Assistance Programs—Prescription Drugs for the Uninsured
PatientAssistance.com
A database of over 1,000 patient assistance programs designed to help those in need.

Social Security Benefits for People with Disabilities
Disability.gov/benefits
Clear information about how to apply for social security and veterans benefits.

Social Security Disability Help
SocialSecurity-Disability.org
Offers assistance in applying for Social Security Disability or in appealing a previous case.

U.S. Government Benefits
Benefits.gov
A resource to check eligibility for different benefits.

Veterans Benefits Administration
www.VBA.VA.gov
Veterans Benefits Administration provides financial and other forms of assistance to veterans and their dependents.

LEGAL
American Bar Association
ABAnet.org
Find a lawyer.

Do-It-Yourself Will
will.preparecase.com

Elder Law Answers
ElderLawAnswers.com

Estate Planning Organizer
estateplanningorganizer.com

National Family Solutions
NationalFamilySolutions.com
File for legal guardianship.

Legacy Writer
LegacyWriter.com

Legal Zoom
LegalZoom.com

National Adult Protective Services
APSNetwork.org
Report elder abuse.

Rocket Lawyer
RocketLawyer.com

U.S. House of Representatives
House.gov
Contact your congressman.

U.S. Senate
Senate.gov
Contact your senator.

ACKNOWLEDGMENTS

Many individuals deserve to be acknowledged for the support they have given me in life and in the preparation of this book. Special thanks go to: my ninety-year-old adopted mom, Sarah L. Sandifer of Chicago, for giving me unconditional love, respect, and encouragement; John W. Sandifer, J.D., who stands by my side and has supported me throughout my journey; my seventy-two-year-old adopted big sister, Thell Dodd, who has mentored and encouraged me over the past nineteen years; Rev. Dr. Mary Newbern-Williams, my spiritual sister, whom I have known for nearly twenty-three years; Nathan Hare, Ph.D., and Oscar Jackson, M.D., who helped me to understand and walk through my healing process; Ameenah Fuller, M.P.P., who is helping in the mission to improve the laws in the United States that protect the rights of veterans and seniors; and the individuals who shared their personal stories or were interviewed for the purpose of creating this book, including William Davis, Patricia Tyson, and Melissa Harris.

I am grateful to the members of my extended family: Jay and Melanie McClain, Melissa Harris, Joy Williams, Martin Brew, and

Maryam Abrishamcar. Thank you for always being there for me and standing by my side throughout the years.

My deep thanks go to those who have helped me prepare, package, and promote this book. Big thanks to my editor and co-writer, Stephanie Gunning, who helped me to transform my pain into passion in the development of the contents of this book. I am indebted to Lynn Serafinn for lending her expertise in marketing to my project. Thanks to Renee Duran for her cover design. Thanks to Shaila Abdullah for her interior design. Thanks to Jessica Keet for proofreading the manuscript. Thanks to photographer Ron Boily of Winnipeg, Canada, for allowing me to use his image of the white American pelican on my cover, and to photographer Grant Kinney of Oakland, California, for allowing me to use his image of Sonoma Beach State Park under a full moon on my cover. Thanks to William Morton for assisting me with Facebook marketing.

Special thanks (in roughly alphabetically order) also go to:

- AARP Regional Vice-President Rawle Andrews Jr., Esq.

- AARP Legal Department: Tonya Acker.

- AgingParents.com: Carolyn L. Rosenblatt, R.N., Attorney at Law.

- AgingParents.com: Mikol S. Davis, Ph.D.

- Allison Maslan, CEO of Blast Off Business and Life Coaching.

- Bernice Tingle, City Council Member (Mountain House, California).

- Blare Media (Fresno, California).

- Carla Thomas, journalist, *The Oakland Post.*

- Dr. Alissa, FitMind Coaching (Maplewood, New Jersey)

- Fred Elken, Perry Publishing & Broadcasting Company, Inc.
- Sharen Hewitt, Executive Director, CLEAR Project TV (San Francisco, California).
- Tiffany Fitzgerald, TiffTalks Radio.
- Paul M. Sensibaugh, Community Services District (Mountain House, CA)
- Mxolisi T. Sowell, Internet Talk program, Amelia Court House, Virginia.

ABOUT THE AUTHOR

Carolyn A. Brent, M.B.A., is the founder of Grandpa's Dream LLC, as well as Caregiver Story, a non-profit organization that provides free medical and legal resources to the public. Her personal mission is to enhance the lives of family caregivers and their aging parents. As a speaker, she travels throughout the United States lecturing about the importance of adult siblings and parents having what she calls "crucial conversations" in preparation for the end-of-life issues they may face, so that instead of being torn apart, they can come together as a strong family. As a result, they can create a supportive and loving environment that a parent needs in order to depart the world with dignity.

Carolyn's passion for her subject started when she was caring for her own father, who was diagnosed with dementia in 1997. From that experience, she found that neither she nor her family truly understood not only the medical challenges related to aging and chronic illness, but also the financial and emotional weight these bring to bear on a family. In 2009, she founded her business, Grandpa's Dream LLC, and the non-profit organization Caregiver Story for the dissemination of information through books, speaking engagements, and a web-based info portal, with the hopes of them becoming instruments of positive change for other families experiencing the same pain and heartache she experienced, and who were being challenged by the need to plan for their aging parents' medical, financial, and legal well-being.

Carolyn's professional background gives her rare insight into the medical side of these complex issues. For seventeen years she worked for some of the world's leading pharmaceutical companies. She served as a clinical education manager for Pharmacia, in which capacity she worked with some of the leading and key opinion leaders in the medical field. In her role as a senior therapeutic sales representative for another major pharmaceutical company, she provided information to doctors and staff on a variety of subjects, including medical healthcare plans.

Carolyn has worked as a volunteer within different assisted-living facilities, including the San Joaquin Behavioral Health Evaluation Center. Since 2008, she has volunteered her services to the United States Congress, working toward making the Veterans Administration responsible for upholding the decisions veterans have made about the appointment of a financial fiduciary and medical representative, in the event of their disability and protecting those whom they select. Her goal in life is to empower caregivers and their family members with knowledge of possible challenges they might face together while caring for an aging parent.

Carolyn received a B.A. in Business Administration from National University in Los Angeles, California, and an M.B.A. at the University of Phoenix, in Pleasanton, California. She currently resides in Northern California.

CPSIA information can be obtained at www.ICGtesting.com
Printed in the USA
BVOW07s2219250115

384921BV00001B/8/P

9 780615 475011